LIFE ABSOLUTES
Thee Instruction Manual For Life

$[(e^E)\ T]A = \text{Outcome}$

Author Karen LaVoie

Life ABSOLUTES ~ Thee Instructional Manual For Life

Copyright © 2006 by Karen LaVoie
All rights reserved.

Second Printing

Illustrator: Karen LaVoie

Editor: Kelly Jo Horton

Published in the United States of America. No part of this book may be used or reproduced in any manner whatsoever without the written permission of the publisher and or author.

Publisher: Copper Sylk

ISBN: 1-893879-25-9

WGA-West 1165649

Manufactured in the United States of America

To God, my Eternal gratitude, love and service.

To my parents YOU are the best.

My eternal thanks and love to my parents, family and friends…you know who you are!

To ALL of YOU.

God bless YOU with a Perfect Life!

Love Always,

Karen

CONTENTS

ACKNOWLEDGEMENTS..vii

FOREWORD

    PURPOSE OF THIS BOOK......................................viii

MY GUARANTEE..xi

CHAPTER 1: MASTERING YOUR WORLD

    YOUR MASTERY IS WITHIN 1

CHAPTER 2: ENERGY-LIFE FORCE

    IN THE BEGINNING 5

CHAPTER 3: EMOTIONS-LIFE'S POWER

    THE TRUTH REVEALED 7

CHAPTER 4: THE LAW OF ATTRACTION

    YOUR ENERGY, VIBRATION AND ATTENTION 21

CHAPTER 5: THE FREEDOM OF CHOICE

    PERCEPTION 29

CHAPTER 6: SELF MASTERY CREATES SUCCESS

    IS THIS VALID? 33

CHAPTER 7: ACCOUNTABILITY

Re-qualifying Your Energy ………………………..59

Chapter 8: What Is Your Purpose in Life?

Your Life's Blueprint ……………..……………67

Chapter 9: Where Are You Living?

The Three Cities ……………………………...77

Chapter 10: Timeline

Opposite Worlds ……………………….............93

Chapter 11: Goal Setting And Achieving

Dream So Big It Takes Your Breath Away ………..101

Chapter 12: The Power Of Visualization

Now Is Your Tomorrow ……………………...115

Chapter 13: The Silent Killers

Language And Behavior That Destroys ..………..123

Chapter 14: Validate Me

Someone Please Make Me Feel Important ………...141

Chapter 15: Qualities of The Masters

"Being" —Allowing Perfection To Be ……………145

Chapter 16: The Factor of One

Your Relationship With The "One" ..………………155

CHAPTER 17: COLORS AND MORE

    HOW ARE THESE AFFECTING YOUR WORLD? 169

CHAPTER 18: ATTRACTING ABUNDANCE

    GIVING, OPEN HANDS RECEIVE ………..………………….173

CHAPTER 19: BEING FEARLESS

    THE SILENT POWER …………….……………………….....183

CHAPTER 20: NO SUCH THING AS A SECRET

    ENERGY KNOWS ...…………………….………………………187

CHAPTER 21: MY WAKE UP CALL

    ASKING FOR HELP …………….….…………………….191

CHAPTER 22: IN CLOSING

    A COUPLE OF STORIES ……………………………………..198

CHAPTER 23: Q & A

    LIVE CONVERSATIONS …...……………….....………....199

CHAPTER 24: MASTERING YOUR WORLD PROGRAM

    WORKSHOPS, SPECIAL OFFERS ………………………….205

CHAPTER 25: RESOURCE GUIDE, REFERENCES AND MORE 207

CHAPTER 26: ABOUT THE AUTHOR …………………………...209

CHAPTER 27: QUOTES AND SAYINGS THAT INSPIRE …………211

ACKNOWLEDGEMENTS

I dedicate this book to all of those who have walked the path before me. Thank you for leaving pebbles and boulders along the way to mark the path. Thank you for whispering in my ear, shining your light before me and thank you for the few and "necessary slaps upside the head." I am eternally grateful.

To my parents who said I could be anything I wanted to and allowed me my own life lessons without the *"I told you so's."* I am eternally grateful.

To my clients who have allowed me to live my purpose in life through coaching. I am eternally grateful.

To my school teachers who cheered me on, especially my fourth grade teacher Mrs. Essinger, who inspired the passion to learn in all of her students and encouraged me to reach my potential. To Mr. McGee, my sixth grade teacher who understood my desire to be the best I could be.

To the United States Twirling Association of which I was a member and competitive baton twirler for 10 years, thank you for your time, dedication and efforts. Some of my best life principles were learned during this time of my life. I still live by them and teach by them. They say golf is the game of life…well, so is baton twirling!

FOREWORD

Purpose of This Book

Note from the Editor: If you're a professional New York book editor or one of my former journalism professors, you're going to cringe at some of the punctuation and sentence structure in this book. I too am a student of the *Associated Press Style Guide*, but I had to let that go when I edited this book. Why? Because Karen LaVoie has a unique personality, and a unique style of communication, and I want you to feel that when you read the book. Those of you who have met Karen know exactly what I am talking about. When you read this book you hear her voice. This book is not about perfect grammar and perfect punctuation. It's about <u>your</u> perfection.

First of all, this is <u>not</u> a Quick Fix formula. It is a <u>proven formula</u>. You will actually change many things about yourself through disciplines that will create **masterful** new habits that work!

How do I know what I say works? Because the formula and truths I share in this book saved my life! One night in dark despair, wanting to no longer live, I screamed out, ***"GIVE ME ANSWERS OR TAKE ME OFF THIS EARTH!!!"*** My cry was answered in that very moment of letting go. The insight that came to me for months afterward is shared in detail in this book. I include the complete knowing of the Law of Attraction in these truths and more.

As much as you love to figure things out yourselves, sometimes a little expert guidance is the catalyst you require for personal and professional growth, more prosperity and better health.

Would you like to walk the talk...Master the Universal Laws of Life and...

- **BE** MORE JOYFUL
- **BE** MORE WEALTHY
- **BE** MORE HEALTHLY
- **BE** IN THE CAREER OF YOUR DREAMS
- **BE** MORE SELF-SUFFICENT

- **BE** FREE OF TIME
- **BE** MORE SELF-CONFIDENT
- **BE** IN GOOD RELATIONSHIPS

You have always been in charge of your world. It's time to...

- BE SUCCESSFUL • BE PASSIONATE • BE THE RESULT • BE VITAL • BE INSPIRED • *BE ALIVE AND BE YOUR TRUE SELF NOW!*

Listen to your inner voice and allow yourself the freedom and experience to achieve your goals and desires. YOU are reading this because this is what you wanted yesterday...let's make it happen.

Start mastering your world today. *"It serves no one when you play small, SO BE BIG."*

I challenge you to greatness. To master your priceless gift!

Let's get started! I'm here today to share with you the program **Life ABSOLUTES**^{TM} ~ *Thee Instruction Manual for Life—the Law of Oneness.* All of us desire to be in charge of our lives, and all of us desire to be able to get out of life what we really desire. And we've been told that we can have anything that we desire as long as we go after it. And at some point in time, we wake up and say, *"Wow, how come I'm not getting what it is that I desire to the extent that I desire it?"* Or, maybe you realize, *"I'm getting what I desire, why does that keep happening? It must be luck."*

Some of you are already quite successful in every facet of your lives, and this book will explain to you why that is, and how to stay on that successful journey and not sabotage that success down the road. I'm here to share with you today the TRUTH that YES, you can have what you desire in your life by finding out what really makes you happy as a being, as long as you work with the Laws of Life. What I am going to share with you will go against some information you have heard before. **Remember, some very well respected experts once thought the world was flat!** Stay open to this information. Some of you might realize by the end of this book that your marriage, your job, your career, might not be the place that you're supposed to be in. You might discover that maybe you're supposed to be a in a different career. Live in a different place. This journey is about discovering what really, really makes you happy in life. A lot of you are going to remember why you love doing what you do at your "job", what you love about your spouse, why you took that job, why you got married and why you are so doggone thrilled to be able to be here. Re-visit those passions in your life, and start living through those passions. Get yourself excited about getting up in the morning again, and doing what it is that you love doing. Discover why it is that you do what you do, and why you have those passions, and how you can keep those passions, those powerful tools in your life, and let the other things go. Discover how to regain your health and self-esteem. Rediscover YOUR Passion for life! YOUR Purpose. Finally, **YOUR instruction manual for life!**

TRUTH: Every day we have a choice of how we're creating the world that we live in, and we've had that opportunity ever since (eternity) we were born. And most people are just kind of going through their life making choices and living with the results that are happening in their world. *"Oh, well—that's the way life is."* You are allowing yourself to be a human pinball bouncing wherever you are slammed, pulled or hit.

I'm here to tell you that you do have control over what happens in your world, over what materializes in your world and over the choices you desire to make in the moment. You have complete control over where you desire to go in your life, in your finances, in your personal relationships, in your health, in your business—everything that you desire to achieve and everything that you've ever desired to have. Stop letting your life control you. I'm going to give you the TRUTH and the tools to be able to create the life you desire. It is up to you to re-learn them, apply them, gain the knowledge-knowing, except that wisdom and use that mastery.

By the end of this book you will be saying, *"I always knew this!"* Now I know it, believe it and live it! I am the master of my world!

MY GUARANTEE

I know that what I offer in this book works. I know this because of all the successes I have had with clients since 1997, and the successes I've had with myself. The knowledge, wisdom and mastery I offer works when used. YOU must use it, apply it, accept it and acknowledge it—then allow it to work. It saved my Life!

The changes in your life will be significant and amazing. Some say, *"Miraculous"* This is not a Quick Fix program. This book has the formula for how one manifests, attracts, creates and keeps abundance, joy, good health and freedom in one's. It is YOUR choice. It will take discipline, dedication, determination, love, forgiveness, compassion and yes, application.

I created this program in the hopes of helping everyone avoid human suffering and limitations and to empower you to be all that you were created to be, do and have. This one formula covers relationships, career, health, finances, abundance and the personal self adding up to you mastering your world.

Feel free to highlight materials, underline key points and keep track of your *AH*HA* factors in your *AH*HA Journal*. Please be patient with *You*. It took time to get to where you are now and it will take time to return back to your perfection. It will be well worth it. I guarantee it. Remember to celebrate every victory big or small. That is part of the moment building of this program.

> *"Wake up and live the life you were blessed to live—instead of the one society says you should."* - Karen LaVoie

> *"Man must cease attributing his problems to his environment, and* **learn again** *to exercise* **his will** *and his* **personal responsibility."**
> -Albert Schweitzer

Mastering Your World

CHAPTER 1

MASTERING YOUR WORLD ™

YOUR MASTERY IS WITHIN

"The truth shall set you free." —Jesus. You are now prepared to learn this important life changing information. Perhaps you've already heard some of it in bits and pieces. Some of the terminology that I use might be different than what you're used to. All I ask is that you keep an open mind. Read from your heart. Set your ego aside. You will be amazed what you re-learn and or remember... you have always known these truths. This program is simplistic, precise and clear. Welcome to **Life ABSOLUTES** ™ **~Thee Instruction Manual For Life.**

TRUTH: Mastering Your World -That's what we all desire to do in reality. We desire to be happy in our lives. We desire to get up in the morning and feel and say:

> *"I love what I do in my life. I love my career. I love the relationships that I'm in. I love where I live. I love the family and friends that I have around me. I love my health. I love everything that's around me. I love the money I have, and everything else I'm ALLOWING to be better, and I'm at peace with that!"*

Mastering our world is really what every single one of us desires to be able to do. We desire to be able to have the perfect life that we were told that we could have. We were told when we were younger, *"If you work really hard, and you're a really good person, then you should be able to have all these things in your life."* At some point in time you wake up in your life and you say, ***"Why? Why am I not getting some of the things that I really desire?"***

Maybe some of you are in a place where you really, really are very happy with what you have and you desire to stay on track. You

Life ABSOLUTES

desire to have more. I am here today to share with you how that works.

TRUTH: There are laws in the universe that are in place whether you consciously know about them or not, and I'm going to explain them to you today.

Keep in mind my quote; *I am the outpicturing of my emotionally driven thoughts and actions.* This is what I am going to talk about—**Life ABSOLUTES.** *Outpicturing* is the outcome, end result, of what you have created in your world. It is your view of your world.

TRUTH: There are laws in the universe: they do not change, they are immutable. Once you're aware of what they are, it will be so much easier for you to be able to live your life, be able to enjoy the relationships that you desire, enjoy the abundance that you desire, and enjoy the joy and happiness that you desire. When you choose to gain mastery of these laws, you will then master your world. Note: So-called *human laws* are really just agreements because they can be broken. Universal Laws cannot be broken. When you attempt to break them, they break you.

"I am the outpicturing of my <u>emotionally</u> driven thoughts and actions." Emotions are the key component to mastery. Understand that YOUR emotions drive your thoughts and your actions which create the world you're now living in. I realize most of society has been told otherwise. Let me prove this TRUTH to you.

TRUTH: EMOTIONS are your power. Go into the space of pure love, joy, bliss—the quiet space where you have NO mind chatter. The place of only feeling Divine Love. Go there. I'll wait……you are back, Ok. No thoughts, correct? CORRECT.

Now have a thought without any feeling. Go ahead…you CANNOT. Feelings come first! The saying you might have heard, *"As a man thinketh, so is he."* which lead people to believe it is our thoughts that create. The completed version of the quote is, *"As a man thinketh in his heart, so is he."* This is the completed version of that quote. "Heart" is feeling/emotion. The Law of Oneness is the Law of Love—the causeless cause.

"All Power is within and is therefore under our own control."
-Robert Collier

Each and every one of you, whether you realize it or not, are in control of what happens in your world.

TRUTHS RECAP: $[(e^E)\ T]A=$Outcome
- There are Universal Laws that are immutable and once I know them it will be easier to work with them.
- Emotions are the key component to mastery.
- The Law of Oneness is the Law of Love.
- _____
- _____
- _____

"I was so happy with the results within myself I wanted to share with my entire staff what Karen had to say. The impact on the employees was incredible. It really made them dig deep within themselves and ask the questions...Many employees made significant changes in their life. Some stopped unhealthy relationships. Some prioritized their life and some just started loving themselves and their families with all their heart. As a gift I gave each employee the opportunity to have a one-on-one session with Karen on my dime to learn more about themselves.... I recommend everyone do this for their employees. It is an investment and it definitely sends a message you as an employer care. It goes a long way."
-Cindy Witcher, LA-Z-BOY of Oregon

"I finished your book yesterday. I have to tell you that I loved it. I found it brilliant and genius. Even stranger, I had started to hear and learn about the law of attraction a month or so ago and then there was a portion in your book about it. I found that to be ironic and interesting that I attracted this concept into my life.

Life ABSOLUTES

Simply a fascinating topic!

Everything you write about is so accurate, it makes total sense and it registers like a ringing bell. It's familiar, in some way. It's like you have all the answers and they are coming from this very high source in the universe, or even from g-d or angels. Incredible! When I read the book I felt so giddy and happy, I noticed after each chapter I felt more positive, safe, resolved and clear. Since reading your book there have been changes, some important "family" ones that I hope are going to be for the better. I sort of knew about colours but you explained it so beautifully and clearly, so much makes sense now, and I now understand why your book is white. But Karen, you get it; you know the answers to life and YOU REALLY ROCK!!!"
-Erin Weinstock

"*Your book is more addicting than chocolate! I read it every day and refer to it quite often so I keep it with me. The best book since the Bible."* -Jean Mark

Sometimes you **feel** like you're not in control of anything, I am going to explain to you in the coming pages how and why you are in control and how you can take more control of what you're doing without interfering with other people's lives. **Let's start with you mastering the knowledge of Energy-Life Force in the next chapter!**

Energy – Life Force

CHAPTER 2

ENERGY - LIFE FORCE

IN THE BEGINNING

TRUTH: In the world, there is a source that gives everything life force—energy. Energy—Life Force is what makes everything in the world function—it's what makes everything in the world exists. There is energy that flows through you as an individual. Your body has energy running through it at every moment of every day. It's the only way that your hands can move, your feet can move and your body can function.

The empty space we call air is energy. A chair is solidified energy. Everything in the universe is made up of energy. So knowing that everything's made up of energy means that you are tied to everything that is VISIBLE and INVISIBLE. Now, that energy is pure and it's perfect and—guess what?—that life energy flows into us. <u>It flows into YOU!</u> And that energy flows into you and allows you to have emotions, thoughts, and to have spoken words/actions, and it then allows you to be able to fulfill the dreams and desires you choose to have in your life —YOUR world.

So you have this perfect energy. This means in reality, with that pure perfect energy flowing through you, you should have perfection in your life at all times. Right now you might be saying, *"Hello! Mine isn't that way!"* So what's the story? How did I, our society get these things in the world that aren't so perfect in appearance? Answer, YOUR emotions. Period. Plain and simple.

TRUTHS RECAP: [(e^E) T]A=Outcome
- Everything is energy-life force and that energy is perfect. That perfect energy flows through me giving me life.
- _____
  _____

Life ABSOLUTES

- _____
  _____

Emotions – Life's Power

CHAPTER 3

EMOTIONS ~ LIFE'S POWER
Energy qualified with Emotions + Thoughts + Action = Outcome

EMOTIONS

That energy I mentioned that flows through you, flows through what's called your emotional core before it leaves your body. The emotional core is located in an area called the solar plexus. Remember that energy is pure when it hits the emotional core in the human being. What happens in the emotional core is that energy gets qualified with constructive emotions (positive emotions), or qualified with destructive emotions (negative emotions). So we have positive and negative emotions as human beings. YOU have emotions qualifying YOUR life energy! Formula: Energy (E+T+A) =Outcome

TRUTH: This is the Law of Energy and Vibration. Emotions are vibrations. Every emotion has it own unique vibration. More on this later. Stay with me.

Think of your emotional core as an onion, and in the center of that onion, there's a little final core. The very center of that onion, the final core, is the pureness of who you are in the center of that emotional core—Divine Love—Oneness. There are many layers on your emotional core that build up over time. We build those layers around our emotional core because we've been told, *don't do this, don't be this way, you can't be that way, you're going to fail, you're a loser, you're pathetic*…tons of "negative" input from yourself and others. Or maybe you've been hurt or are afraid. All of these "experiences" that are destructive have built layers around your emotional core over time, and those layers eventually start shutting you off to your pure emotions. The more layers you have, the farther away you are from knowing your real emotional core. You can remove those layers! Pay attention to your emotions, they are your alert system to what's going on in your life!

Life ABSOLUTES

Our emotions are at least four times more powerful than our thoughts! It is said that 70% of our energy used to function is emotional. Your emotions alert you to whether you're making a constructive or positive choice in the moment or whether you're making a destructive or negative choice in the moment.

The emotions that you have are the key essential element of the human being, but you've been told by society to squash them. *"Quit crying right now. Suck it up and move on. You don't have time to deal with that. Move on."* The only emotions you are permitted to experience are **happiness, fear, hate and sometimes it's OK to love**. Those are the paltry few acceptable emotions that society says we can have, unless we pay $9.00 or more and go sit in a dark room and watch a movie with a whole bunch of strangers. Then it's OK to have our emotions, and we cry and we laugh and we can experience the range of emotions that have been buried inside of us. We then walk out of the theater and pretend it never happened. Humans are emotionally driven. That is why we are constantly seeking stimulation, the roller coaster ride—the highs. You will realize by the end of this book that you want to get off that emotional roller coaster ride.

TRUTH: Emotions are the number-one way that we communicate. Think about it. You travel to a foreign country and they don't speak your native language. You can still communicate with people. You communicate through emotions. Everybody's experienced emotions. We also know that sometimes what comes out of a person's mouth really isn't the honesty of what's being said. We know what the truth is because we can "sense/feel" their real emotions.

TRUTH: Emotions are the truth of what's going on in an individual's world. No matter what the words are saying, the truth is what's happening in the emotional core.

Let me remind you that emotions are the most important element of the formula to mastery. Are you ready to stop hiding them and suppressing them? I would like for you to start acknowledging that you have emotions! Sometimes, this might be a bit of a challenge,

Emotions – Life's Power

because people haven't been taught to acknowledge their emotions. The only way you can start using your emotions properly is to acknowledge the emotions that you have experienced. Once again, let me remind you—**emotions are your alert system.** That's how you create things in your life. That's how you are communicating with other people. That's how you do your job. That's how you have relationships. Remember, energy is pure and it's perfect. So every day you get up, you have GREAT odds of being very, very successful, because that energy that's flowing through you is perfect. You have an excellent opportunity to go out and have a terrific day based on your emotions being constructive—positive.

How many people are aware they have emotions? OK. I think we're all aware we have emotions, and you **now** realize those emotions qualify your life energy with either a positive quality or with a negative quality. And that's your choice. I will talk about choice later.

How do you qualify that energy that's flowing through you, with a positive emotion or with a negative emotion? First, to help you to understand how emotions work—please do the following exercise. **Exercise #1:** Get out a piece of paper and write in a column the numbers 1 thru 20. Now write down the names of the emotions that you know that you have experienced as an individual in this lifetime.

Writing a list of your emotions is probably the most challenging thing I'm going to give you to do. Stop reading and do this exercise now. Spelling is not important. Start writing. Stop when 5 minutes is up or when you have finished. Thank you.

Are you done? **Really?** GOOD. NOW READ ON. I'm going to give you a little hint.

TRUTH: There are over two hundred emotions in the human, way over 200.

You might have been able go on and on and on. Or you might have stopped at emotion number three. And that's kind of an example of

Life ABSOLUTES

where we are as a society of human beings. We have been told from the time since we were knee high to *stop having this emotion, stop having that emotion, don't do this, don't do that, don't be this way, don't be that way.* And so **the acceptable emotions in our society are love, fear, hate and sometimes it's OK to be happy.** Those are the acceptable emotions that we can have, because you're not supposed to cry in public. In reality you're not supposed to have love in public because, *"ooh, that's gross."* We can hate and we can argue. We can kill, fight, yell and steal in public. That has the appearance of being OK.

Why should YOU be aware of the emotions that you experience on a daily basis? Why? **They are the alert system within the human being.**

TRUTH: YOUR emotions tell you how you're ruling your world, how you're creating in your world.

A lot of people take their emotions and squash them and basically sweep them underneath the rug. From today forward you want to be aware of what emotions you are experiencing. What will happen is that six or seven months out those squashed emotions will finally erupt and the human will have this outburst, and the human won't know why it just had that emotional outburst which in reality had been controlling what had been happening in the human's world for weeks, perhaps months!

Remember, (repeating myself) the human emotional core is like an onion. And those layers have come from fear, doubt, pain, selfishness and from lies. We bury, and we layer, and we cut ourselves off as an emotional person for one reason or another. We've been rejected, we've been told 'no' one too many times, we start shutting down and cutting off our ability to be one with that emotional core of oneness and we shut ourselves off from knowing what emotions are going on inside of us.

Here is a sample list of emotions:
1. Happy

Emotions – Life's Power

2. Mad
3. Sad
4. Fear
5. Adulation
6. Anger
7. Jealousy
8. Pride
9. Yearning
10. Hate
11. Tenderness
12. Excitement
13. Joy
14. Love...*why is this so far down the list?* — Most people interviewed placed it this far down the list. *Curious. Yes?*
15. Impatience
16. Envy
17. Grumpiness
18. Elation....*That's just happy isn't it? No, it's a different form of happy. It's a different level. It's a different level of happy.*
19. Security
20. Lust

Peace, Hope, Bliss, Hurt, Overwhelmed, Sorrow, Anticipation, Vengeance and Worry.

These are emotions that perhaps exist within you at some point in time in your day...at some point in time in your life? And we have all kinds of other emotions. I mean there are hundreds and hundreds and hundreds of emotions that work within the human being. We are constantly being driven by emotions. How these emotions affect your world is very, very, very important. Some of these emotions are extremely positive, and some of them are what is called negative or destructive to the world that you desire to live in. They're destructive to your health, to your relationships, to your job, to your finances, to the happiness that you're seeking. How many of the emotions that you wrote down were positive? How many were negative? In an unscientific study, I have noticed the clients that have more negative emotions than positive ones on their list are the ones with the most "garbage to clean up" in their lives—the most lack and limitation.

Life ABSOLUTES

Once again, that energy, which is pure, is Divine Love. **When I say 'love' it's not romantic love, it's the love that—you just love something—unconditionally.** Divine Love is unconditional, but people like to say unconditional love so I'm going to throw that out there for clarification.

You have the opportunity to allow love to flow through you in every moment of every day. Let's say you begin your day with that pure energy flowing through you, into your emotional core. At some point in your day you experience the emotion of hate, and then later on in the day you experience the emotions of joy and happiness. Those emotions you experience during the day affect how your energy goes out into your world, and how it gets created in your world. One big roller coaster ride!

Image 2

So how do YOU get those emotions in your emotional core?

Emotions – Life's Power

TRUTH: You get emotions through your five senses: sight, hearing, touch, taste, and smell. Your senses put your attention on a person(s), place, thing, condition, conversation, inner dialogue or whatever is in your environment. All of these things create emotional responses within the body. The two senses we use the most are sight and our hearing. So, when you're looking over there putting your focus or attention on something, and it gives you an emotional response of, let's say, happiness...

1) You have your energy being qualified with a positive emotion; your emotional response is *"I feel happy."*
2) Energy is qualified with a positive emotion which triggers positive thought, which then triggers *"I'm happy"* a thought which triggers...
3) A positive action, thus resulting in a...
4) Positive "happy" ending.

Life ABSOLUTES

FORMULA: energy qualified with a $^{+\text{(positive)}}$ Emotion, triggers a $^{+\text{(positive)}}$ Thought which triggers a $^{+\text{(positive)}}$ Action which creates a $^{+\text{(positive)}}$ Outcome. **[(energy$^{+\text{Emotion}}$)$^{+}$Thought]$^{+}$Action=$^{+}$Outcome …human in the flow.**

When you put your attention some place else, and you see something that triggers fear, you have the same formula—just replace the word positive with negative, and that energy then that flows through you gets qualified with fear, and creates more fear in your world.

FORMULA: energy qualified with a $^{-\text{(negative)}}$ Emotion, triggers a $^{-\text{(negative)}}$ Thought, which triggers a $^{-\text{(negative)}}$ Action which creates a $^{-\text{(negative)}}$ Outcome. **[(e^{-E}) $^{-}$T] $^{-}$A=$^{-}$O**
when Emotion is negative then the Thought, Action and Outcome are negative.
(e x $^{-}$E) x T= $^{-}$eET
$^{-}$eET x A= $^{-}$eETA
$^{-}$eETA = $^{-}$Outcome…human with resistance.

Let me explain yet another way…
Every emotion has a vibration to it. The more pure/positive/constructive the emotion is, the higher the vibration. The emotion qualifies the life energy that is flowing through you, through your emotional core, and then goes out and attracts like a magnet all other life energy of the same rate of vibration —give or take a few rates. **(See diagram below.)**

TRUTH: Life energy always returns to its creator, like a boomerang. It flows circularly. Image 4

As your Positive energy flows out into your world it collects/attracts more positively qualified energy, thus raising its rate of vibration, and returning to you—its creator—something positive, as long as your energy is still in that rate of vibration. Otherwise, it waits until you are in the same rate of

Emotions – Life's Power

vibration again, which opens the door so to speak, for it to come back into your life. This is known as "being in the flow"...*I'm on a roll! I keep receiving all these great things coming into my life!*

Example: you can be in a "bad" mood and get around a group of happy people and shift into happy, thus allowing that vibration into your life by your choice, or you can stay in a bad mood by choice. It is easier, and requires less energy to be in a good mood, thus the greater absorbing the lesser, or the greater raising up the lesser (the greater always assists the lesser in life. You do that every time you allow yourself to have positive emotions.) YOU do that for all of mankind.

It is just the opposite for negative/destructive emotions. The flow of negatively qualified life energy is known as *spiraling down*. Less and less positive life energy...less "positive" things in ones life.

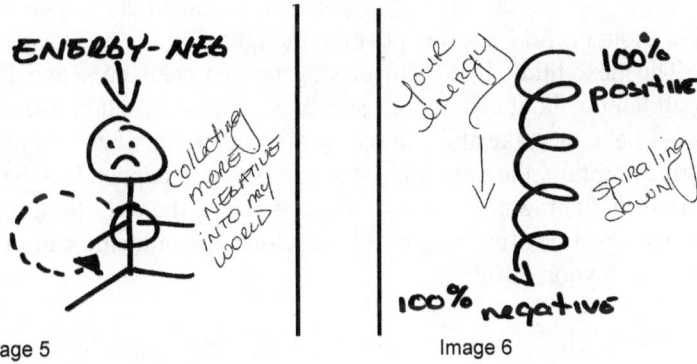

Image 5   Image 6

Your life energy qualified with positive emotions is shown as a water faucet with water flowing...gushing powerfully when your emotions are positive, thus allowing perfections to be, to flow. Image 7

Life ABSOLUTES

However, the faucet turns almost completely off when negative emotions are qualifying your life energy—this is the choking to death expression, the pushing away of the good, the repelling of good, otherwise described as *being out of alignment with life or turning your back on God...stepping out of the light.*
Image 8

Once again, understanding you have energy that's qualified with emotions and from emotions you have thoughts. Take happiness for example. You have happy thoughts which result in actions, and from those actions you have what you created — your end result—happiness, which is positive. Say, *"I just feel happy today. I'm going to make a cake!"* That's a positive thought. So I get this positive thought, *I'm going to make a cake!* The next thing I do, I'm mixing up the cake mix, and I'm being all happy about this action. So I have a positive action, the end result is I have the cake and I'm happy about that. So when you have a positive emotion, the only thing that can possibly happen is to have a positive thought. And from a positive thought, the only thing that can happen is a positive action. So therefore, the outcome can only be positive in your world.

In somebody else's perception/world, that cake might be evil! It might be, *"That's the worst thing you could have possibly done because I don't want that cake in my life"* and to you it made you happy. So in your world, creating that cake was a very, very positive thing. That is called perception...choice. Freedom of choice.

TRUTH: You came into the world with one knowing, that was love. As I have stated, the human being has five senses: smell, sight, taste, touch and hearing, and those senses trigger the emotional core. The outcome, the end result being, energy having been qualified with **emotionally driven** thoughts and actions. You have an outcome.

Emotions – Life's Power

And here's what I'm here to share with you—what has not been taught to people is this: when your emotions are positive, you naturally have positive thoughts. You stay on those positive thoughts, which can then only result in a positive action. And the only possible end result is that you have a positive outcome. That's the ultimate way for the human being to live. That's the perfect way to use that energy that flows through you, always qualify it with positive emotions. Period. This is known as "Oneness."

TRUTH: When you only have positive emotions going on in your body, the only thing that you can have in your world is perfection. So, I'm here to tell you that through ignorance, disobedience, fear— EGO, as human beings—we've been allowed to have destructive/negative emotions. We've been told it's OK to have negative emotions. It's OK to be angry; it's OK to hate; it's OK to be sad, and have negative emotions. What nobody ever told us was what the end result of that thought process would be. What happens when you have a negative emotion, and you allow it to stay a negative emotion? You then have a negative thought, which then, based on the intensity of the emotion causes a negative action, and the only outcome can be something which is negative/destructive. That's the only possible outcome you can have—should you not **negate the formula through choice…Freedom of choice.**

FORMULA: [(energy ^{Emotion})$\Rightarrow$ Thought] $\Rightarrow$ Action $\Rightarrow$ Outcome
[(e^E) T]A=O

TRUTH: Your life energy is moldable to whatever quality you impose upon it. It is easier to be positive /constructive than it is to be negative/destructive because it takes less exertion. Re-qualifying your life energy as negative is like swimming upstream—the ole going against the flow —the "Hitting your head against the wall." Ouch!!!

When you go with the flow, you have more powerful, sustainable energy (for example, when you are happy as opposed to when you are depressed or angry). You have more sustainable, energized, reusable energy when you are positive. Whatever the quality of the

Life ABSOLUTES

emotion, that quality is the guaranteed end result of the <u>completed</u> formula.

TRUTH: EGO is that which FEARS, doubts, lies, steals, deceives, cheats and is pure negativity. There is NOTHING good in the EGO. **Fire it!** EGO is the opposite of love.

Let's review. Emotions are what allow you to create in your world. Emotions are what give us that creative power in our world. Emotions are 70% of the formula...OK...I'll give you the rest of the breakdown—thought is 17.5% and an action is 12.5%. Amazing! How much energy do you appear to be using running around getting "nothing" done? Why does it appear that way? Check the emotion driving your thoughts and actions then you will become an amazing time manager!!! People are amazed at how much "successful" people do in a day. That is because they are working with the Laws of Life.

So, your life energy that is innately positive is ready to be shaped, molded into whatever your heart desires. By putting your attention on something, you create an emotional response, which triggers a thought, which triggers an action, which creates an outcome. The outcome is the same as the cause. Cause and effect. Positive to positive. Negative to negative. When I say positive or negative, I mean the rate of vibration. Likeness. Commonality. When you have complete mastery you only have cause, the causeless cause. There is no longer the cause and effect process if you will.

That's the way you are creating in your world. You do it every day, in every moment. You are doing it right now. YOU might not acknowledge that you are "conscious" of it. Start being conscious of your choices. Your ego will lie to you and say you are not responsible for the things in your life. That is called denial. The blame game—the pity party—that is called fear, doubt and selfishness. *"I'm just going to be a feather on a breeze going wherever the wind emotionally blows me. It's not my fault...."*

TRUTH: You know that there are consequences to your actions, which means—there are consequences to your emotions! Let's treat

Emotions – Life's Power

the "cause" and stop attempting to fix the effect. Sound familiar?

Let's go to your source of power—your emotions and gain mastery!

The first emotion was love. Love is your starting point. (see diagram below). The further away from love you get the closer you get to negative emotions, or destructive emotions. Destructive emotions are: fear, hate, pride, jealousy, rage, anger, sadness. You may be familiar with a lot of these emotions because they feel uncomfortable.

TRUTH: Fear is the creator of all destructive emotions. Fear is the lack of love of self. In reality there are no negative emotions when you use them as an alert system...they all become a part of the knowing, *"It's All Good."* Everything helps you to be a better person and eventually you will have only love in you! For now let us look at the example and be aware of the not-so-positive emotions that are your alert system to STOP and make a better choice! ☺

LOVE—Positive/constructive emotions
.
.
FEAR ………………….. **(Invisible line)**
.
.
Numb
DEATH of the Physical body–flat line

We have love. We have passion not lust. We have happy, we have joy, we have elation, we have peace, we have harmony—we have all of these positive emotions that we can choose from.

OK, now we have an idea of some of the emotions that run through us as human beings. The very first emotion being love, in reality, I say the other emotions are sub-emotions of love or lacking love. However, I will stick with all of them being emotions just to keep it simple for this instruction.

Life ABSOLUTES

So the true self innately centers, longs to be in a state of "love." That's its natural state, where it likes to function. Once again, I'm talking about pure love—Divine Love. The real self likes to be in that place because everything in its world then comes into place, the way that it should be—Divine order—because it has love acting through it in every moment of every day creating or allowing that perfect world that the real self desires to live in and create. We are co-creators or creators whichever one works for you. They are both true.

You might have heard Divine Love expressed as joy, bliss, happiness…in reality Divine Love is Greater than the aforementioned.

TRUTHS RECAP: [(e^E) T]A=Outcome
- Everything is energy-life force and that energy that flows through me is perfect, and it flows through my emotional core before it leaves the body I have.
- My emotional core: Emotions are the truth of what's going on in my world. No matter what the words are saying, the truth is what's happening in MY emotional core. Emotions are my alert system. MY emotions tell me how I am ruling my world, how I am creating in my world.
- **Formula: 70% emotions** + 17.5% thoughts + 12.5% actions = 100% outcome.
- I will realize by the end of this book I want to get off the emotional roller coaster ride.

Now that you have a better understanding about the role and power your emotions have in your life, let's add in the understanding of how you actually attract into your life what you want through the Law of Attraction. Next chapter!

THE LAW OF ATTRACTION

CHAPTER 4

THE LAW OF ATTRACTION

YOUR ENERGY, VIBRATION AND ATTENTION

Remember, when you put your attention on something, you're using your five senses all the time. Whatever, you are choosing to put your attention on triggers an emotion in your emotional core. So when you're putting your attention on something that you really like, you're triggering a positive emotion in your emotional core through the vibration of that on which you are putting your attention. Such as, *"This feels good."* Then you think, *"I really like that!"* That triggers you being happy—triggers you being joyous —allows you to stay in oneness with your pure life energy. It triggers you being excited. It triggers you to maybe be in love. Whatever it is, that emotion qualifies that energy flowing through you or allows it to stay "perfect." When it's a positive or constructive emotion, it then flows out into your world. Because energy has to come back to its source/creator/user, it flows out with all of its positive vibration, affecting a lot of people in your world in a positive manner, should they choose to be positive. It's easier for them to choose to be happy when you're being positive. When that energy comes back to you, it comes back to you in a more positive way because it has collected more positive energy on its journey. It shows up as more money, better health, better opportunities, more joy... whatever it was that you were focusing your attention on. Why?

Your emotions, thoughts and actions (**actions include "spoken words"**) have qualified your life energy-life force, and it has gone out into your world and created more positive things that you desire in your world, or "attracted" them to you. So you place your attention on something that you choose to have in your life, and you put out passion about it. You are taking action that is prompted by positive emotions. You have learned to expect something positive in return; you're attracting that back into you like a magnet. It goes out and gets that which you desire in that positive energy and brings it

Life ABSOLUTES

back to you! Attracting that common energy vibration, that common bond...the birds-of-a-feather-flock-together knowing. You are a magnet. It brings back to you exactly what you put out, equal or greater than what you put out. This is why people say the universe is converging or conspiring on your behalf.

For example, you desired to attend college. You were excited about it, and you were positive about it, so you set out to accomplish that. You went your one quarter and you were really positive about it. You went your second year, your third year. You were taking action; you were having positive emotions, positive thoughts, and positive actions. The end result was that you graduated! You got the degree that you desired. That's because you were putting your focus, your attention on what you were choosing, desiring in your life. You were choosing to have this really great, positive thing in your life. You were focusing in a positive nature on graduating. You graduated because your attention was on what you desired and overall you enjoyed the process! Your positive emotions kept you propelled...the momentum going forward. Your thoughts were clear and focused and your actions constructive and purposeful. Image 9

The universe (God) is energy–Divine Love just waiting to be called forth into action. Waiting to be molded and shaped, waiting to come forth from the so-called invisible to the visible. The universe does not know individuality, it only knows vibration. God knows you by the love you sent out, and then in return, returns more love in the manner that fulfills the call(s). Negative does not get to God. God is ALL perfection. Ask and thy shall receive. "Ask" means in a way

The Law of Attraction

that you're "asking" is constructive for everyone. God, which is love, then receives the asking of love (God's pure vibration of energy), thereby receiving his love back, adding to it and in return sending it back again! Thus, expanding it!!! Give and thy shall receive. Give for the sake of giving. NO strings attached. Give unconditionally, for the sake of spreading love. *Just because I can! Just be "cause".* The cause should always be Divine Love.

For every action there is an equal, greater or lesser reaction. (I will address the statement of lesser later on.) When you're positive, you end up attracting more positive people, situations, and things around you. And because energy flows circularly, the more positive you are, the higher the rate of vibration of positive energy you attract back.

Image 10

And for the sake of drawing what energy symbolically speaking might look like, the highest vibration of pure love looks something like the illustration below. It's vibrating just as fast as it can be in existence!

Positive   Vibration
∧∧

The line on the next page, which is almost flat, is what your energy might, symbolically speaking, look like when you qualify it with negative or destructive emotions. Negative emotions slow down that flow of energy through you—it's like you're just choking it off—and by the time it comes out, it's so negative and it's so destructive that it is almost a flat line.

Life ABSOLUTES

Negative vibration

--------~--------~--------~------

In this next diagram you see the energy is spiraling down. This process is expressed by me as, *"for every reaction there is an action that creates an equal, greater or lesser reaction."* Remember we are reactive beings. You *react* through your senses causing emotionally driven thought and actions. Destructive or negative emotions go out and attract more negative energy, thus, creating an equally "destructive" end result /outcome. "Equal" means just as negative as what you originally put out. "Greater" means you receive back a "greater" destruction, worse than you put out. "Lesser" means the returning energy is of a lower rate of vibration than what was originally put out. Less positive means less energy flowing through you period. Think of the heart rate monitor. What does it mean when it flat lines? No Energy in the body. No Life.

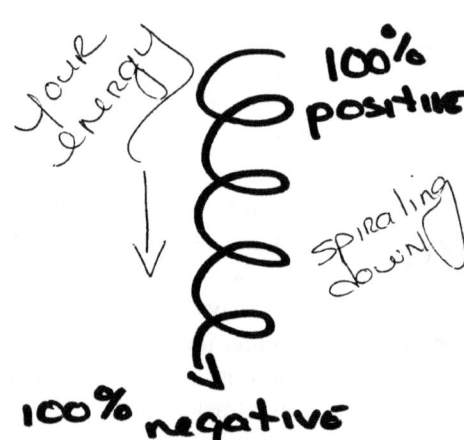

Some of you aren't "aware" of a lot of the emotions that you have because the EGO is suppressing them. When you suppress your emotions for a long enough period of time, you become a great big Walla Walla sweet onion! Your emotional core gets lots of layers. You become numb. You become numb as a being, and that's when you get up and you say, *"Have to go through my day again. I will just go so I can get a paycheck and 'party', 'shop', 'sleep'... on the weekend."*

Things are just kind of—blah—because you're numb and you're not

The Law of Attraction

really having highs and lows; your emotions are just kind of all numbed out and suppressed, because you've been burying everything, *you've been burying everything,* **you've been burying everything**. When a person buries their emotions too far, they may have one emotion that happens to sneak through the "protective" layer and then they snap. They may go out and do something radical that's not constructive, because they suppressed, and they suppressed, and they suppressed, and they can't suppress any longer.

People who continue to suppress stop existing. They're in so much pain and in so much denial that it only takes one seemingly innocuous thing to make them snap. That one little thing makes a hole in all of those "protective" layers—those emotions erupt and that person is forced to deal with those emotions that they were suppressing....which is too much, all at one time to deal with constructively!!! There is very little mastery at this point accessible to the human. You hear people on the news; they interview the neighbor, and the neighbor says, *"She was the quietest person. She never did anything. There wasn't anything in her life that was ever, you know, explosive."*

That is because they were numb. They were numb! What happened is that fear, and that rage, and that anger, and that doubt, and that feeling of worthlessness, that feeling of loneliness, that feeling of sorrow, feeling of pain, just kept piling on and piling on and piling on, and it encased their emotional core. They shut all of their emotions off because they didn't know how to deal with them. And one day, one little thing, something like—the ant crossed over the crack on their sidewalk—and they snapped. And it wasn't about the ant of course. It was more about the last emotion—they couldn't suppress—they couldn't suppress any more emotions. That one emotion they couldn't suppress caused all of the emotions to come out and erupt all over the place.

So you're in a relationship. All of a sudden you're yelling at your partner because he burnt the toast. It really has nothing to do with "toast that burned," and everything to do with 20 other things that built up to that—which you buried in your emotional core.

Life ABSOLUTES

Acknowledging that you are having negative emotions and then handling them, keeps you "above the line" in the positive zone. You want to stay out of the area "below the line", which is the negative, because it destroys your health when you worry, when you have fear, when you have anger. It destroys your health because you're getting indigestion, you're getting stomachaches, and you're experiencing headaches. Your body starts reacting to that negative energy inside. And that negative energy starts tearing your body apart because it likes to be in that pure energy which is love. **In reality human beings like to be in the place of love.**

Is there anybody who honestly doesn't like the feeling of love? NO. Those of you who said yes, in reality you don't like the feeling of <u>not</u> having love—so you say I don't want love at all! So you are getting exactly what you don't like—**the pain of not having love.**

We like being in the place of love. We love to give love, express love, share love. We like how it feels when somebody loves us. We like how it feels when somebody appreciates us. We like that feeling. So as individuals, what every one of us can do, is to choose at every moment how to be in a place of love, joy, compassion or forgiveness.

And so, I'm here to remind you how to stay out of the negative environment, how to forego suppressed emotions, and how to use your emotions in a really, really positive way.

Remember that energy flows circularly, and when you're putting out negatively qualified energy you're attracting back more negative or destructive things into your life, because you are a magnet. The angrier you get, the more garbage in your life you get—the more things go wrong. Have you ever said, *"Why does this keep happening to me?"*

> *"You create your own universe as you go along."*
> -Winston Churchill

TRUTH: The negative results keep happening to you because you're putting that energy out that's qualified with negative or destructive

The Law of Attraction

emotions. And so, when that energy goes out, it goes and collects more negative, destructive situations, relationships, people, health, finances.... YOUR energy is a magnet; it brings it back to you what

you put out—what you put out is what you get back. If that is where you're putting your emotionally charged attention; you're focusing on what you <u>don't</u> desire. What happens when you focus on what you don't desire? YOU attract back to you what your focus is on. That's exactly what you get, because that's where you're focusing your emotionalized energy. That is where you are sending your energy. This is the law of attraction—where you send /focus your emotionally charged attention is what you attract back through your emotions, thoughts and action. Image 11

Life ABSOLUTES

"Insanity: doing the same thing over and over again and expecting different results." -Einstein

Change your "cause"—your emotions—and the outcome will be different! Change your attention. Change your emotion.

TRUTHS RECAP: $[(e^E)\ T]A = Outcome$

- Emotions are what give me the POWER to create in my world. I am gaining mastery over my emotions and where I focus my attention in order to have greater mastery in my world. I am a magnet.
- I am focusing on what I want to attract more of into my life and keeping my attention off of what I do not want.
- I like the feeling of love. I choose to put forth and express the emotions of love, joy, compassion and forgiveness. Suppressing my emotions is deadly. I will be aware of my emotions. I will not suppress them. I will handle them immediately keeping me in the positive zone.
- _____
  _____
  _____
  _____

Emotions are what give you the POWER to create in your world. You must gain mastery over your emotions and where you focus your attention in order to have mastery in your world. PERIOD! Remember, I am a magnet.

YOU have freedom to choose so let's talk about choice!

CHAPTER 5

THE FREEDOM OF CHOICE

PERCEPTION

How do YOU gain mastery over your emotions? At all times in life we have choice, and I know that you've heard this before: YOU make choices in every moment of every day.

TRUTH: YOU have the freedom to make choices and you want to go deeper than that. You want to be making choices at all times about the emotions that you're feeling/experiencing inside yourself or from others. When you have a negative emotion, you are entitled to change that negative emotion and turn it into a positive emotion. You have that choice. **YOU have that choice!** Freedom of choice.

TRUTH: Avoid the Quick Fix. It is the EGO lying to you! Some people say, *"You say it is not good to yell at that person. But it felt good."*

That is a quick fix. It's a quick fix when you do yell because you know in the end that when you yell at somebody, you hit somebody, it might certainly have felt good to you in that moment, but in the end you absolutely know that there's going to be a consequence to that action. It's not going to be a good one. The person who is a drug addict knows when they do that shot of heroin, the end result is not going to be good. In that moment they feel good, but the end result is not positive; they feel worse. The alcoholic, the smoke-aholic, the shop-aholic, the food-aholic, whatever it is, it's a quick fix. Sometimes you have negative emotions, and you have a temporary so-called "feeling of happiness—satisfaction." *"I'm so happy I did that, out of rage."* When you were angry, you felt really good about it. I'm here to tell you that is a temporary fix.

It's a temporary moment of false happiness, because in reality you know that you're going to be accountable for that action that you just

Life ABSOLUTES

took. When you went out and broke out all the windows in somebody's car, it felt really good at that time, but in reality you know that you are accountable for what you did, and that doesn't feel good, especially when you have to shell out a couple thousand dollars to fix the broken windows, and possibly go to jail. For those of you for whom money is not an issue and jail is not an issue...you are lying to yourself! So that quick fix—feeling "high" —is not a positive emotionally driven experience. It's you kidding yourself that there's a positive end result. It's the same quick fix that the addictive personality has, whether the quick fix is alcohol or drugs, or food or shopping, lying, cheating, sneaking, whatever it is, you're not going to be happy about it because the accountability comes back. That means that you went from something negative to negative to negative and you ended up with a negative end result. The "high" was a lie. The high one gets from being on an emotional roller coaster ride is a lie. It is the EGO telling you it is OK to destroy your life. It is your EGO telling you, *"I feel alive."* You feel alive, because you have suppressed so much pain, the human was going numb—choosing not to feel at all. Therefore, any kind of pain/negative emotion makes the human feel alive for the moment because the pain allows the human to know it is still alive ...then it suppresses even more emotions because it cannot deal with the pain it just created. The so called "high" is the lie that you are truly happy. The true high is Divine Love—being in positive emotions. Then the high is self-sustaining. The high keeps feeding itself on more positive emotions! That is the real "high" in life.

All right, I do have a happy ending to this. The happy ending to this is knowing that negative emotions have the possibility of leading to negative thoughts. I'm here to help. You can fix it. I have a solution. When you have a negative emotion in your emotional core, you can feel it. It should be an alarm. **Let negative emotions be your alert system.**

When you're having a negative emotion, your desire should be to stop it, because the end result is going to be something negative. Ask yourself, *"Oh, do I really desire a negative outcome?"* Because that's what I'm guaranteed: when I have a negative emotion, the only

The Freedom of Choice

outcome that I can have is negative, unless when I'm having that negative emotion I say, *"You know what? I choose to change this. I choose to make a choice right now to change that negative emotion!"*

Take your stand! Be firm and happy about that choice! "Magic wand." You are now in positive emotions. Ta Da!!! More on this to come.

TRUTHS RECAP: $[(e^E) T]A = $ Outcome
- I will avoid the Quick Fix.
- I choose to have positive emotions. I have that power and control in my life.
- _____
- _____
- _____

Life ABSOLUTES

- _____
  _____

"Ms. LaVoie, your program Life ABSOLUTES has made the 12 step program that much easier. Your program made the steps more clear, precise and achievable." -Cheryl G.

"LIFE ABSOLUTES Thee Instruction Manual For Life" - written by Karen LaVoie is not only a must read book it is a must use book. Included are insights to being a true master of our own life, confirmation of our purpose, and day to day successful living. My book is already highlighted, underlined and showing signs of use. I highly recommend the truths between the covers of this gem."
-Rev. George Truett Crawford

So how do you switch your emotions from negative to positive? Read on!

CHAPTER 6

SELF MASTERY CREATES SUCCESS

IS THIS VALID?

So how do you stop a destructive/negative emotion, thought or action? How? By asking yourself, *"Is this valid/useful?"*—"this" being the emotions and information being experienced.

Let's say you hear a comment. You sense it with your senses and it causes an emotional response that is a so–called negative emotional response. At this point you're probably not really aware of your emotions all the time so you instinctively don't know what to do yet when you get that, *"Uh oh. This doesn't feel good"* feeling. (Believe me, you're going to become an expert at recognizing the emotions that you're feeling all the time. Your emotions are now going to be this alert system for you) Here's what you're going to do. Whenever you have a negative emotion, you're going to recognize in your emotional core *"Warning! Warning! Warning!"* You're going to stop in your tracks, then ask yourself, *"What I am focusing on right now? Is it not what I desire—obviously, I am experiencing negative emotions, therefore, what do I really desire? Is this valid, is <u>this valid</u> what I heard, I thought or experienced?"* Do you want to be experiencing negative emotions? No. Then the negative perception is not valid for you. Find the positive.

When you catch yourself experiencing anger, rage, sadness, disappointment, anxiety, worry, or fear (any negative emotion), and when you start recognizing those emotions in yourself, you can stop yourself and say, *"Why am I angry? Why am I worried? Why am I afraid?"* And the reason for that is—you're not seeing the truth in what's really going on. Within everything **find the truth.** You can reverse the negative and find a positive. When the focus of your attention is on what you do not want, OK. What **do you** want? Find the "love" in the situation and that is what you want. What are you fearful of? Fear causes all negative emotions. Remember negative

Life ABSOLUTES

emotions are the EGO lying to you. I am going to give an example later.

In the middle of a negative thought, you can change the process. You can stop in the middle of the thought and you can make it positive. You have a choice to stop in the middle of thought. When I was teaching myself this discipline, I would stop mid-sentence. People would say, *"You didn't finish."* I would say, *"Because I know what I was going to say was negative."* Stop mid-sentence; change your emotion, which changes your thought. It's OK. It's well worth it. **It is well worth it!** Because once words come out of your mouth, you don't get to take them back. They're out there. So be very careful of the words that you use, and the things that you say to people.

You can even stop your negative action. By that time, it's certainly more of a "challenging opportunity," however, you can do it. The EGO is really powerful by then. You can stop in the middle of that negative action and decide to make "it" something positive. When you get to end of the formula, you deal with the outcome. You are faced with that negative outcome should you choose to stay in the negative. You live with the consequences of whatever it is that brought "it" into your life. It is NOT worth it!!!

When you have a negative outcome, negativity/destruction shows up in your life as: lack of money/abundance, bad relationships, unemployment, poor health, lack of time, lack of joy, and lack of energy—all the things that you don't desire in your world. The stress that you have, that discontent that you have, that's how you've arrived there, because you were putting out negative emotions, which led to negative thoughts, which led to negative actions and caused a negative outcome in your life. I'm not here to point out that we have faults as human beings; I'm here to teach you, YOU have the power of choice, and the power to be more conscious of this process. You are conscious because you have negative emotions—**This is the Law.** Negative emotions are your proof you are not in obedience with the law.

TRUTH: The Law of Energy and Vibration—the Law of Attraction

Self Mastery Creates Success

is immutable. Ignorance doesn't matter. It doesn't matter that you supposedly didn't know that this Law existed. It still works. It's happening in your world right now. Remember, human laws are not really laws at all, they are agreements because they get broken and changed. This formula is the LAW. It never changes or gets broken. The human laws get broken and changed! I'm here to give you the upper hand, to now be aware of the Laws and NOW make choices to go forward and have the positive things that you desire in your world. Love. Positive Relationships. Abundance. Happiness. Good Health. Prosperity. Freedom. Joy.

"To be wronged is nothing unless you continue to remember it."
-Confucius

Now are you ready to master how you change your negative emotions into positive emotions?

Example: Say something triggered one of my five senses and gave me a negative emotion. Say somebody (she) came up to me and said, hypothetically, *"Hi, Karen, it's really good to see you. What is up with that ugly green outfit you're wearing?"*

As a human being I can say, *"Oh my goodness – I – I! I'm hurt by that!"* You know, that's the knee-jerk reaction of a human being. When somebody says something that could be construed as *mean*, automatically one gets angry. That's 'kind of' the human reaction. I'm going to be on the defensive and I'm like, *"It isn't ugly!"* In reality, I have a choice, and everybody else has a choice, when somebody says something to you and you take it in as a negative, you can say, *"OK. Does that have validity in my life? Is my outfit ugly? Gosh it is! Thank you for telling me."* Thus, "magic wand" I am now positive.

"It is the mark of an educated mind to be able to entertain a thought without accepting it." -Aristotle

So what I perceive as a negative actually becomes a positive, because I realize the truth of the situation. *Hmmm, perhaps I*

Life ABSOLUTES

shouldn't be wearing this outfit and nobody else had the honesty to tell me that it is one ugly outfit that I am wearing. So it is valid.

Say it isn't valid?—I like what I'm wearing. You know what I say inside my head? *"Fine, that's her/your opinion."* Everybody is entitled to their opinions. We have a world that is living proof of this.

We drive different cars. We wear different clothes. We eat different foods. We like different movies. We like different music. We're entitled to our own opinions. So it's her opinion, she doesn't like the outfit, OK, *note to self: maybe don't wear green suit when I come and see so-and-so.* Because to me, I still like my outfit, so I'm still happy. I'm happy that I know that it's probably not the best outfit to wear around her, but I'm still happy that I like my outfit, so I'm still happy. It didn't hurt me. I made a choice not to let it hurt me. I say out load, *"Really, you think so?"* and say OK. And move on. In reality does it really matter? Is it valid? Is it worth being upset about and attracting a negative outcome over? NO. Nothing is worth experiencing negative emotions. Period.

The third thing that one can do is say to that person, *"Really you think so?"*—this might give more insight as to why the person said what they said, and allow the "letting go" and or help you discover the positive in what was said. Should the situation keep bothering you for a really long period of time perhaps you should let the person know in a non confrontational way that what they said hurt your feelings.

You can have a calm response, so that you don't allow people to constantly injure you. People think that you <u>have to</u> stand by and let people injure you. You're entitled to say something, the point is, say it in a positive way.

You can't/won't be happy when you stay in that place of negative energy. I mean, come on, I get to control my life—I want to be happy. So the only way that I can be happy is by addressing whatever hurt me at that time, as soon as possible, from a place of being calm, a place of finding out how can I make this a positive for

Self Mastery Creates Success

me? What was the message in this situation? Was this valid or not?

The message might just be, *"That person doesn't like green suits. OK. Life goes on."* It doesn't destroy my world unless I allow it to destroy my world. It will destroy my world should I choose to walk around being angry about the green suit comment, which means the rest of the day I probably won't do a whole lot of anything that is productive because my energy will be focused on the comment about the green outfit. When I choose to stay angry, I am giving my power away to the other person. Somebody half way across the world doesn't care whether my suit is green or not. It doesn't affect anybody but me. My energy does—but not the suit. So by holding onto that anger, all I'm doing is destroying my world. I'm taking my energy and destroying my world, because you can bet that person who made the comment moved on. They're out doing whatever they're doing; they're out riding their horse having a good time and I'm still angry about the green suit making my day a bad day, because I chose to make it a bad day.

What **I know now** is that I have choices. When somebody says something to me that hurts me in my emotional being, I can say, *"Is that person's opinion valid in my world? Does this green outfit look ugly on me?"* Well, perhaps it does look ugly on me, and then I say, *"That was really nice of them to say that. They were being honest and they told me, so I'm grateful that they told me."*

So my emotion becomes positive because they actually were doing something helpful. Their opinion had validity for me. **It had validity for me.** So I stopped that knee-jerk reaction of being on the defensive because they told me my green outfit looked really ugly. I have stopped being a defensive individual and I have started saying to myself *does this have validity in my world?* As human beings, we have been trained to be on the defense. Make the choice to stop being a defensive person. Stay in the happy zone. Stay in the harmonious zone, and when information comes in to you, question the validity of it.

So—the outfit doesn't look good on me; I agree with that comment,

Life ABSOLUTES

so I'm happy that somebody told me. What if I think the outfit looks really great on me? I'm still not going to be hurt, and you know why? That's their opinion and they're entitled to it. They're entitled to their opinion, because each and every one of us has freedom of choice.

> *"Holding on to anger is like grasping a hot coal with the intent of throwing it at someone else; you are the one getting burned."*
> -Buddha

TRUTH: YOU have freedom of choice. You have freedom to decide how things affect you in this world. You have freedom to decide which actions you're going to take in your life. You have that freedom. Knowing that you have consequences for every emotion, thought and action that you choose and the consequence can be constructive or it can be destructive. YOU have a choice of how to react when somebody says something to you: you can get defensive, feel hurt, or ask yourself, *"Does that have validity?"* Maybe your inner voice says, *"That's their opinion and I still like the outfit and I'm going to wear it. It's all good."*

Now the opposite is: I can get really angry because I can allow that to hurt me. I can put my attention on the ego feelings, *"Oh, that was so mean and that was so wrong,"* and get really worked up and have that negative emotion(s) just running all through me, qualifying my energy, and then causing me to have negative thoughts and actions.

So, I'm really angry: *"Fine! She doesn't like my green suit? I don't like her car."* So I go out and start breaking the windows in her car. I keep breaking them! So what's the end result going to be of that? I'm going to be accountable for that action. I might end up in court, I might get arrested, and I will end up paying her for the windows that I broke, because I allowed that negative emotion of anger to take me over, and I went out and took the action of breaking the windows out in her car. The fear that I am not good enough in her eyes or fear she might be right caused that anger, the fear of not being loved-accepted.

Self Mastery Creates Success

So we have a choice as individuals. YOU have a choice. I have a choice. When she says that to me, I have a choice: Do I desire to be angry or do I desire to be positive? I can choose to be positive, and so I will ask myself,, *is what she said valid*? Is it valid to me? I'm not asking whether it's valid to her; I'm asking whether it's valid to me, because I'm mastering my world. Is it valid to me?

And I say, *"I like my green suit. It's just her opinion."* And I go on and I'm still happy with my green suit. It's just an opinion. I can choose not to be angry. I can choose to say, *"You know what? That's her opinion and she's entitled to it. That's great."* And I'm still happy. I don't go out and break any car windows. I don't get in trouble. I just move on. **It's not earth shattering. My world doesn't fall apart.** I didn't allow that split–second choice of anger destroy my world and move me into actions I would regret later.

What happens when it doesn't have validity and I'm not able to just say, *"That's her opinion?"* In the beginning of this new way of living life, every once in awhile, there might be one of those "things" that just kind of hangs in there, eating away at you. This is the result of the ego having a conversation in your head that keeps going and going and going and going. So when you don't address it, for the next hour, you're saying, *"I can't believe she didn't like my green suit."* It's just like—I like my green suit. *"Look at all the clothes she's worn! She's worn that red one. She's worn that brown one! And I don't like those, and do you think I told her that? I didn't tell her that!?"* You could go past that negative emotion into the negative thoughts and really start getting the ole negative emotions cranking—the ego "loves" to have those conversations in the head. The ego gets really good, and gets witty and sharp, and has those negative conversations. We have these argumentative conversations in our heads a lot of the time that give us more anger, more frustration or sadness because we keep processing it through our intellect. Now it's up in our brain which is very smart and knows how to run five billion zillion miles an hour and it can run that same conversation for at least a month. You know, it's really good at it. You might be laughing right now at yourself and that is good. Everyone has done the above in his or her lifetime.

Life ABSOLUTES

So for the next hour or three hours, the next month, sometimes for the next year, you still have that anger at that person and it's built, and it's built, and it's built. And guess what's happens? All that energy that was flowing through you, that you could have been using constructively—you wasted it! You're wasting it on a conversation that you're having in your head and you're not being productive because of that. All or part of your focus is still on the choice that, *she didn't like the green suit*, and you didn't get very much productivity done in your day, month, year… because you had that distraction. You had that continuous conversation going through your head around and around and around. It's an endless tape that goes around and around. Gathering more momentum—doing more destruction in your life.

And here's the comical thing that we do as human beings. We get in an argument with a person in our head. They're not there. You're having this argument with YOURSELF.

Example: Me, *"Well you know I really like this green suit and since you are my friend, you would say that you like it."*

Then I **play** "her": *"But I am your friend and that's why I told you I didn't like the green suit, and by the way, I don't like the brown shoes that you wore with it either."*

Then me, *"I can't believe you don't like my brown shoes!"*

When we have the argument with the other person, we never win. **We never win.** Do you ever notice when you're having an argument in your head with the "other person" that really isn't there that you never win? You don't! You don't even give yourself a break! You always make that other person wrong so you can keep arguing. YOU'RE never happy. That's because you have so much pride/ego that doesn't want to just let it go. Let it go!!! Is life about winning or about being truly happy?

TRUTH: Find a way to resolve your negative feelings and thoughts, your perception and let "it" go, by doing so you won't be defensive

Self Mastery Creates Success

in your head conversations…as a matter of fact, better yet, YOU will stop arguing in YOUR head! YOU will stop having "head" conversations that waste your time and energy!

So you want to allow yourself to have resolve. Resolve your so-called issues A.S.A.P.

TRUTH: It really is that simple, but the human has really become addicted to being in negative energy. We've become addicted to arguing, to being angry, to being upset, to being sad—we've got an addiction to the roller coaster ride—the false high. The lie you "have to" have the bad in order to appreciate the good. LIE! Good gets better and better…use this formula and you will discover it for yourself. You can break that addiction. How? Every time that you feel negative emotions stop them by using the formula—not sweeping them under the carpet or burying them. Allow yourself to find resolve and move on. And then you're going to get hooked on being happy. Being joyous. Being free of all the fears that you've been carrying around. YOU do not need the negative in order to enjoy the positive. Yet, another lie of the EGO! You will soon realize "it is all good". This is not an "out" for not being accountable for your mistakes in life. Correct your mistakes and then move forward. This is the way that life expands itself into greater perfection.

When you use the formula—you're having emotion, you have thought, you have action—in the middle of that emotion, you have a choice to stop that negative emotion. You have a choice. That's why I state—be aware of the emotions that you are experiencing. They are your alert system. Your emotions alert you to whether you're going on the right path of what you really desire to create in your world or whether you're destroying your world. Positive, constructive emotions allow you to create everything you desire

41

Life ABSOLUTES

in your world. Image 13

When you're having negative, destructive emotions, you're destroying everything around you. You're destroying your health. You're destroying your relationships. You're destroying your finances. You're destroying everything around you. That's why negative emotions are destructive. They destroy—lower vibrations of energy, when left to go lower, implode on you—self-destruct. When negative emotions are never fed again they disappear. Puff!

Back to the example conversation—so in the middle of that emotion of anger you can say, *"Oops! Warning! All right. I'm focusing on the feeling/perception that she doesn't like my green suit. I'm going to put my focus on something positive."* What would be a positive thing? *"It's her opinion"*—moving on. Note: This is not an out to **not** listen for the truth. When you say, *"That's her opinion"* and still have negative emotions…you did the formula incorrectly.

Take your attention off of what was causing a negative emotion and put your attention on what's going to be positive. Take your attention off of what is making you angry. Take your attention off of what is destroying your world and put it on what is constructive in your world. Put your attention on the solution….not the problem. Put your attention on what you DESIRE.

Note: The solution is in the problem—don't like being fat? Take your attention off of "being fat" and put it on being healthy, become healthy! Focus on healthy!!!

Sometimes you're already into the thought. It's going in your head, and you can feel that emotion. Your chest starts hurting; your stomach starts tightening up sometimes, because your emotional core is telling you, *"Warning! Warning! Warning! Stop! Stop! Stop!"* You can stop that thought.

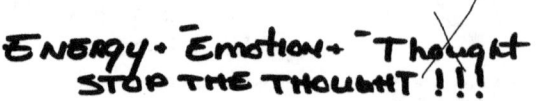

Self Mastery Creates Success

Stop the thought and put your attention on what it is that you desire. You know what you don't desire. So STOP and figure out what it is that you do desire. You're changing your focus. Take it off of what you don't desire; put it on what you do desire.

In the middle of that action, you can still stop and make a choice. I'm out breaking the windows out of her car and when I get to the third window I can say, *"Oh my goodness"* and I can stop. Instead of paying for four windows, now I only pay for two. That really is a positive thing. It's the ole silver lining in everything. So in reality, there is a positive to that because I'm only paying for two windows instead of four.

You can stop in the middle of an action. Now this is where ego really comes in, because people are in the middle of the action and they don't want to admit that they're making a choice that they really shouldn't be making. They don't want to stop in the middle of that action. But I'm here to tell you, it's better to stop in the middle of that action, and be embarrassed because it is only your ego. It's a more positive choice than following through, because when you stop at this point, the outcome can be changed. You still have a chance to change the outcome.

When you don't take the opportunity to take that negative outcome and turn it into a positive, that negative energy keeps going and going and going and going until you resolve the choices that you have chosen that are destructive. Accountability—cause and effect is not a religion—it is the LAW of Attraction—Energy and Vibration.

Should I get to the end result which is negative—guess what? I still have the choice to make it right. Before they find out that I broke a window in their car, I can go, and tell them, *"Don't be surprised when you see your car there's a window broken out. I did it. I'll pay for it. I apologize. Please forgive me. You know, it was a moment of—well, I had a serious lapse in judgment, I should have made a better choice, however, I didn't, so I want to make it right."* You have the opportunity in life to make those things right, that you know, for you, were destructive or negative.

Life ABSOLUTES

You can fix what you have done. This is a really, really powerful realization. Once you start catching yourself in the action of doing something that you didn't consciously choose to do, I want you to celebrate! Yes, celebrate every time you discover that you're in the action of doing something you shouldn't be doing, celebrate that you caught yourself because maybe you didn't catch yourself before. It means you're getting better at being able to make positive choices. Instead of being angry at yourself or frustrated with yourself, that you caught yourself in the middle of something negative, celebrate it. This is good. So catching yourself in the middle of the action of doing something negative is like, *"OK, I am getting better! Victory dance!"*

Next time, what happens is you catch yourself in the thought process. **You** catch yourself in the thought process. And it's even more celebratory because you say, *"Oh, that is so great I caught myself!"* It's so much easier to stop in the thought process than in the action process. I'm now catching myself having the negative thoughts, and I'm changing them. **I'm changing them!** You get really, really good and realize when you're having negative emotions. Remember, be patient and yet, stand on guard. The momentum will keep building. Be disciplined, dedicated, determined, and obedient and apply, apply. Allow these laws to be your mastery. The proof is in the outcome. The proof manifests in your world.

As an individual, you have your own world and you have energy that flows through you and that energy always stays within the world that you create and goes out into the rest of the world. Say you have 65% positive energy in your world and 35% that is negative or destructive. That energy flows through you and you choose to do something positive, it is now 76% positive and the negative is now 24%. YOUR world is getting better.

You're in the flow!

Self Mastery Creates Success

Image 15

Ever have those days where everything's just clicking? Everything's good. I'm having a great week! Life is good! Work is great. My family's good. My finances are good. My health is good. Whohoo! <u>I am happy!</u> That is "being in accordance" with the LAW! You are being in alignment with your natural state of positive energy.

Whether you know it or not, in every moment in every day you are "in agreement" with the LAW or in opposition to it. This is what you're doing. You're making choices, every moment of every day, you're making choices. That's what you do—choices, choices, choices, choices, choices, choices, choices. And they're driven by emotion.

When you're really passionate about something, your emotion is very strong and that's why you get results really fast, because there is so much momentum behind it. Your emotion is the power that drives it. When you really don't care about anything, it can take 10 years to get here, or it may never happen, because there really wasn't enough

45

Life ABSOLUTES

power behind it for it to be created in your world. Your emotions are the power behind your focus/attention and your focus/attention is your magnet.

Reminder—always recognize your emotions are your alert system. **Emotions are the alert system.** You have energy. See the drawing as 3-D.

Here's 100% positive energy; here's 0% positive energy. Energy flows circularly, so the more positive energy you put out—and energy always comes back to its source—the energy goes out, and just like a magnet, it collects more positive things. That's why **your** world keeps getting better and better and better.

And when your world starts falling apart around you, it's because you've put out negative emotions, thoughts and actions, and now it starts coming back to you. And it comes back worse than where you were the day before or perhaps the hour before. And your world starts falling apart in a hurry sometimes, because you had one month where you went to town being negative. You get it back and it's like somebody hit you upside the head and started destroying your world. All of a sudden you lost your job, you have bad health, your relationship falls apart, you're broke, and you can't figure out why that happened. It's because you put it out into your world, and now it came back. You go on a tangent for a month or two, and then you really get it back in a huge lump sum. People experience that because they get big wake-up calls when that happens. What happens to most of us is that we destroy our lives little by little, and we don't even recognize we're doing it. After a period of time we look back at our life and say, *"Hey, what happened? My life is miserable, ugh...*

Self Mastery Creates Success

what happened?!"

Now, the great thing about the Law of Energy and Vibration is we have a choice to change the way that the formula is going. We do it every day, we're making that choice. What happens is when you have that energy flowing through you and when you qualify it with a positive emotion, that energy flows out and it comes back to you. Energy, when it's positive, has to flow up. Because when something is positive, it attracts more of what is like itself. When positive energy goes out, it collects more positive energy so when it comes back to you—that's the end result—you get something equally positive or even more positive than what you started with. You have raised the rate of vibration of the energy, or in reality you have allowed it to be more perfect. So when you get on that roll, and things are going really well, you say, *"Oh my goodness, this is so good; things are just clicking! This is really good!"* Because you're in that positive place—and it keeps coming, and it keeps coming, and it keeps coming. Because you keep allowing your life energy to be more positive, this has action, which has a positive outcome.

On the other hand, what happens when that energy comes into you, and you're choosing to be angry? That energy is negative so it has to spiral down, because when you put out negative energy it goes out and attracts more negative things in your world. Because it attracts what is like itself. When it comes back to you, negative or even more negative than where you started—thus, lowering the rate of vibration of your energy.

So, on a pie chart you're at 65% positive energy, and you do something positive,—this is a hypothetical pie chart.

When you're 65% positive, you put something else positive out and it comes back to you, 65% is now, hypothetically, 67% positive in your world, and the negative number changes to 33% negative. But you do something that's negative, because you're angry and you go out and have an angry action, what happens is, the positive is now only 63% positive, and the negative is now 37% negative. So you're affecting the RATE OF VIBRATION OF THE ENERGY in your

Life ABSOLUTES

world, whether you're having a positive day, whether you're having a positive week, a positive month, a positive year, a positive moment, by the choices that you're making. Choices based on your emotions.

TRUTH—emotions are the key factor. Emotions are the power behind this energy that drives the thoughts and actions and compels their outcomes. Image 16

One more time, as a human being, you have five senses. You have taste, touch, smell, sight and hearing. Through those five senses, you put your attention on something. You taste something; your attention is focused on that taste. You see something; your attention is focused on what you're seeing. You hear something; your attention is focused on what you're hearing. You're focusing on something that's positive, and then you're having a positive emotional response, which drives you to positive thoughts and they drive you to keep taking positive actions, which is creating all these wonderful, positive returns in YOUR life.

EMOTIONS ARE MY POWER!

So I'm looking at something that, *"Oh my goodness that is so beautiful. I really like what that person is doing."* And that inspires me to take a positive action and go over and tell them that I like what they're doing. Or go over there and praise them. Or maybe I desire to be like them and have them be my mentor. *"Can you show me how you're doing that?"* So that's a positive action, which then causes, in my life, an outcome that's more positive. It's causing me to raise-up into being a more positive person. I am allowing perfection to be.

Self Mastery Creates Success

Why do I say raise up? Remember the numbers? I go from 65% to 67%...raising my energy rate of vibration. Why do I say allowing perfection to be? Remember, life energy is perfect before it gets re-qualified with emotions from your emotional core.

And the human being is drawn naturally to that place of love. It naturally goes back to that centering. When you stop the thoughts in your head when you're angry, or you're upset, or you have doubt, or you have fear, or you have hate, when you stop the thought process and just quiet yourself, you'll center right back to that place of love. You'll center right back there.

"If you train your mind to search for the positive things about other people, you will be surprised at how many good things you can observe in them and comment upon." -Alan Loy Mcginnis

I'm here to remind you that you have a choice regarding what you listen to and view. There's a lot of destructive music out there. There's a lot of destructive programming on T.V., and in films. I'll tell you, I'm in the entertainment business, but I'll say it anyhow—stay away from the destructive programming. Whether it's real, it's a movie, or whatever it is, I tell you what, you're watching it and your emotional being doesn't know that it's not "real." You're still putting that emotion out into the world. You watch a movie that makes you angry; you're creating that in your world. You're watching a movie that makes you sad; you're putting that out into world. You watch a movie that makes you happy; you're putting that out into your world.

So I watch movies that are very uplifting, very positive, so that I make sure that I am putting out positive, constructive things into my world. I choose to not watch all this media stuff where there are all kinds of murders and negative things going on out there. It doesn't mean that I stick my head in the sand like an ostrich. I'm aware of it, but I don't keep my concentration on it five hours at night, watching the news . You're excessively inundating yourself with the negative. You're pulling yourself down. When somebody passes away—like Princess Diana or John F. Kennedy Jr. —you could feel the energy in the world shift, and it was like this mass suppression of the energy

Life ABSOLUTES

in the world. You could feel it, because a huge portion of the world population had focused their attention watching that. A lot of the people of the world were watching that news that was being fed to us non-stop for days on end, and you could just feel it. 9-11 happened; you could feel that energy, I mean you could just walk through it, because so many people were watching it, over and over and over again. Yes, we want to know what's going on in our world. Be aware. Find a positive. Move on. Stay out of the negative!

When those kinds of situations happen, find the compassion, find the gratitude, and acknowledge the things that you can do that are positive out of that situation. The old saying, *"There's always a silver lining in everything,"* is true. It is true. Stop listening to sad songs, angry songs. STOP. When you do, your life will keep getting better! YOU will find yourself saying things like this, *"You won't believe what happened today! You know how I was talking about how I wanted 'such and such' in my life? Well, John over here just talked to me about it. He knows somebody who will help me! Wow!" things are just coming into place!"* This is the Law of Attraction.

"Karen LaVoie coached me back into my power within an hour and I immediately experienced the love and joy that's always there when we allow it. I am grateful to have experienced Karen's love and up lifting energy." Love and blessings, Terry Ellis, California

That's because you're a magnet of positive energy attracting back to you that which you desire, and by putting out that positive energy, all of those other people with positive energy start attracting to you. You're a magnet for positive people to be around you. You get happy. You have happy people around you. Successful people. (Not necessarily rich people.) Successful people—notice who their friends are: other happy people. Other happy people! Go figure.

When you choose to stay in fear, in rage, in hate, in anger, that's the energy that's flowing through you. It's as though you're taking it and you're choking it off. You're choking, *"Ack! I'm so angry at the world!"* By the time you squeeze it, the line is flat. You squeeze the

Self Mastery Creates Success

life right out of it by qualifying it with anger and rage. The only thing it can bring back to you is more frustration in your life, more anger in your life, more hate in your life, more doubt in your life. You feel lonelier. You feel more worthless. And the whole thing is that it's your perception. It is <u>your</u> perception. Change your perception by changing your emotion by changing your attention.

Just when you think you're down, life kicks you again. You know why? —because you put out negative energy and you keep choosing to see through negative eyes. You brought it back to yourself. You're attracting more and more negative people around you. You're attracting more and more negative things to happen in your life, because that's the signal that you're putting out. I want to be negative, so bring me some more negative. The next thing you know, you're in a pity party with all the people complaining about the same things that you're complaining about. The Pity Party Convention. The people in the pity party are the people who say, *"Well, you know it's Jim's fault and it's Terry's fault and it's Suzy's fault. This is not my fault that I got fired. It's not my fault that I got divorced. It's not my fault! It's not my fault! It's not my fault! It's not my fault!"*

TRUTH: It **is** your fault. It is your fault that you made the choice to bring all of that into your world. You made that choice to put yourself down here at 10% positive energy. You made that choice. Day after day, hour after hour, wherever it may be, you've purposely put out or allowed into your life negative energy, negative emotions, negative thoughts, negative actions, and the only outcome that it will produce is negative. There isn't any other way. It's scientifically proven; it's the way the law works. At any point in time, you could have stopped and changed the process and started going back up. But a lot of people like to have pity parties and blame the world for their failures. Oprah is an EXCELLENT example of a person who did not have a pity party for herself—or when she did it was not very long. She stepped up to the plate and said *enough is enough!* In my opinion ☺ I applaud her!!!

How do you know whether you're creating negative energy in your world? Well, you start seeing a lot of stuff in your life start to fall

Life ABSOLUTES

apart. That's the first sign. You start having relationship problems, that's a sign. You start having financial problems, that's a sign. Your health is getting worse, that's a sign.

Catch yourself saying, *"It's everybody's fault—it's everybody's fault why these things are falling apart in my life."* You can stay on that spiral until you hit rock bottom. You will hit rock bottom and say, *"Oh, my goodness, I need to fix my life; I'm in such a disastrous place."* You can choose to start going up just as easily as you chose to destroy your life. You <u>can</u> <u>choose</u> to be constructive in your life.

How do you get into those destructive modalities and how do you get back to those positive places? Notice where you're focusing your attention. It's all a result of where you're putting your emotionally driven attention! Put your attention on a choice that is constructive in your wanting. What positive things do you choose to have in your life? Put your attention on that. Put your attention on the things that you want in your life. Put your attention on things that make you happy in your life. Put your attention on things that you choose to fulfill—your dreams and passions that you have in your life. Because when you're putting your attention on what you want, I tell you, the rest of the world can be in chaos, but it doesn't rock your world because your attention isn't on the chaos. I'm not saying that you're an ostrich with your head in the sand. I'm saying that focusing on what you want with your positive emotions and thoughts, and following that through with action creates the positive outcome you desire.

What happens when you put your attention on that which you feel and think is negative, that which you're not happy with, or you're angry about? You're experiencing more of that in your life because you're putting your energy there, it's like a little magnet, it's just going out and pulling it into your life. **It's sucking it into your life**. Example, the best way to destroy a really good relationship is to start focusing on the one little thing that you don't like about that person. Spend enough time focusing on that one little thing and it will destroy your relationship. If it doesn't destroy your whole relationship, you'll end up discovering five or six more things that

Self Mastery Creates Success

will. In reality these things might not have really existed until you started focusing on them and or you began driving the person crazy enough that they started doing them!

So the way to have a productive, successful, abundant, joyful life is to focus on the things that you want in your life, the things that you want to create in your life, and take your attention off of the things that you don't want. It's OK to know what you don't want and then move on. OK? I don't want this in my life, so what is it that I do want? OK, I don't want this; this is what I want. Put your attention on what you want then you start attracting it and allowing it into your experience. Feel excited—joyful about what you have your attention on.

Sometimes it is good to know what you don't want in order to choose what's going to make you happy. But don't dwell there. Don't dwell there! A lot of us tend to dwell on what happened last week, a month ago, a year ago, when we were five years old. You're still focusing on whatever that was that was negative or destructive in your life, by your perception. You're still focusing on something you perceived at the age of five to be terrible. You're not going forward creating positive, constructive things in your life because you're still focusing on what you don't want with negative choices. And so that stays with you every single day in your life. And it's there, and it's still there, and it's still there, and it's not going to go away until you stop putting your negative emotional attention on it.

As individuals, it is important to decide to forgive. Maybe somebody in your life, in your perception, hurt you really badly. Be willing to let that go and forgive that person because I'm here to tell you, every single one of us is on this journey every single day, striving to do the best that we can do. That person who hurt you is probably not even thinking about it anymore. They have so **"moved on"** in their life, and you've held onto it for a week, for a year, for 10 years, destroying your life. When you're focusing on the negative things in your life, you don't have time for the positive things that you could be creating in your life. You're not focusing on the things that can make you happy. You can forgive that person who hurt you, and

Life ABSOLUTES

forgive yourself for holding that person in that place and having that energy for all that time. Just walk away from it and say, *"You know what? I'm moving on. I am moving on. I'm right here, right now enjoying my life."*

Image 17

Was it valid? You don't even know whether it was valid because it was so long ago! You don't even know "where you were at" at that time. So you just move on. You can have forgiveness, and you can have compassion. Maybe that person was in a worse place than you were in your life and you didn't know it. And you didn't know it, because you didn't know what was going on inside of that person emotionally at that time. Maybe they were down and had been kicked one too many times and they came across your path. And you got the end result of them being kicked the last time. And they didn't really mean to direct it at you; they were just striking out and didn't really mean to hurt you. When people are hurt and when they're angry, what they're doing in reality is they're reaching out to get love.

Self Mastery Creates Success

When you have hate, and when you have fear, and when you have anger, and you have jealousy, what you (the human being) really want is love. That's what the human being really wants. But you're so far away from love. Love is up there, and you're way down here. You desperately want to get back to love, but you've "forgotten" how to get there. Image 18

Solution—focus on what you want; it keeps you in the positive. Focus over here on what you want. It is like changing the channel on your T.V. or radio station. You are changing the signal you are sending and receiving. Change the signal you are putting out! I appreciate perfect health—then focus on the perfect things about your health. Because the more you focus on what's perfect with your health, the more perfect your health becomes. That doesn't mean you ignore the lesser things. You acknowledge the lesser and you move on and say, *"OOH, OK this isn't working. This is what's going to be perfect about it. I know I don't want this. OK! Now I'm going to stay over here and focus on this. This is what I'm going to focus on. I'm going to focus on what is good. This is a better choice. "I'm going to allow my positive emotions to motivate me to take action."* Image 19

Life ABSOLUTES

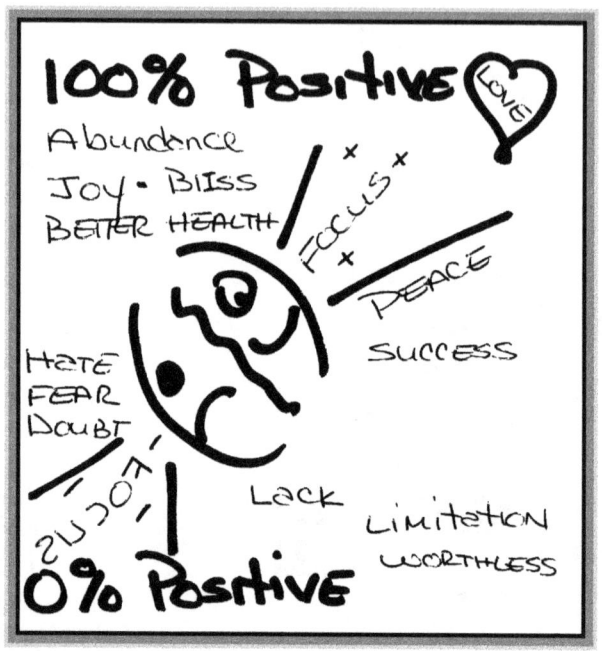

TRUTH: When you're in a relationship, in the beginning everything's wonderful! We focus on all the positive things about that person. Stay focused on the positive things about the people in your life, because then, not only are you happy being around them, it helps them be more positive about themselves. When you're constantly pointing out the good qualities in somebody else, it allows them to be a better person. Let's say, you start taking your focus and putting it on what you perceive to be negative things about somebody, and start complaining. All of the sudden, you took that little molehill and you made it into the biggest mountain in the world. That's all you see about that person. Your focus goes off the positive, and the next thing you know, you can't find a single thing you like about that person. They disgust you; you hate them. But three days, three MONTHS, three YEARS before that, everything in the world was positive about that person. It's because of where you put your attention. It is where you put your attention! You can apply this to your job, any relationship that you're in, any family member, your finances, whatever it is that you want to change. You want to

Self Mastery Creates Success

focus on what it is that you want/enjoy. When you focus on what it is that you want, those positive things you enjoy, then your attention isn't on the negative, and you're not drawing those things into your life. You're not attracting those people or situations into your life.

Your emotions, thoughts, spoken words and actions are the "pulling-attracting" magnetic Law of Attraction. "Pushing" against that which you do not want only "pulls-attracts" those qualities to you more! **Formula of Life:** $[(e^{+E})\ ^{+}T]^{+}A=^{+}O$

TRUTHS RECAP: $[(e^{E})\ T]A=\text{Outcome}$

- **I have freedom of choice.** I have freedom to decide how things affect me in this world. I have freedom to decide which actions I'm going to take in my life. Knowing that I have consequences for every emotion, thought and action that I choose and the consequence can be constructive or it can be destructive. I have a choice when somebody says something to me whether I'm going to get defensive or whether I'm going to be hurt, or I ask myself, *"Does that have validity,"* or I say inside, *"That's their opinion. It's all good."*
- **I can't/won't be happy when I stay in that place of negative energy.** I mean, come on. I get to control my life—I want to be happy. So the only way that I can be happy is by addressing whatever hurt me at that time as soon as possible, from a place of being calm, a place of finding how can I make this a positive for me? What was the message in this situation? Was this valid or not?
- I am going to forgive myself and others so I can move on and be happy.
- _____
  _____
  _____

Life ABSOLUTES

A **powerful** way to gain your mastery even faster is to journal ALL your AH*HA moments. Here is a look at my useful AH*HA JOURNAL. It is actually Gold and white in color. You can purchase it on my website.

Do you want help getting more clarity for what you want and what you are really attracting into your life? Want to help your employees, friends or family members? I offer individual or group workshops and mentoring. I offer retreats, corporate training...*ask me! I travel the country.*

Office: (503) 312-0913

Email: coach@masteringyourworld.com

Accountability

Chapter 7

ACCOUNTABILITY

RE-QUALIFYING YOUR ENERGY

So you are in your world now, being all happy, making positive choices. Be aware! I get this comment on occasion (in fact I got it from myself many years ago), *"Well, Karen, negative things still keep happening in my life. I am being all positive—what gives?!"* Guess what? The "negative" was already there, but you didn't even notice because you were so burdened down by the five bazillion negative things that were going on. Now you have the mastery to re-qualify that energy and move on.

Image 20

Now when a "negative" appears in your life, say, *"Hello, I recognize you, my human created you...you are my misused energy coming back in this 'package' or my attention must be on you right now <u>accepting</u> you into my life."*

Life ABSOLUTES

What is happening is the more positive you get—you're cleaning up your world. You're cleaning up your world! **Yippee!** CONGRATS!

Image 21

Victory Dance!!! You have more skills now to clean up your world. You might not have recognized the negatives were there because you didn't have the skills to deal with them. You didn't have the skills to deal with all of them. So, in reality, it's like the sliver you get in your finger, and finally it's festering up so you can get rid of it. So, you're becoming more positive, you're getting positive! This big ugly negative thing comes into your world that was that sliver that finally festered up. You have the skills to say, *"Hello!"* and get rid of the sliver out of your life. You can get rid of it. So celebrate every single time a perceived negative thing comes into your life, because you're whittling away at the old and you're raising your vibration! Creating NEW POSITIVE HABITS.

You're getting better and better skills to make your life the place you

Accountability

want it to be. That's positive. I celebrate every single time a so-called negative thing comes into my life, because now I have a chance to fix it, should I choose to fix it. I FIND THE BLESSING and move on. My alert system is powerful.

I mean those emotions just become so strong within you. You should be aware of every single emotion. I'm here to tell you, as you get more positive, you're going to say, *"Oh my goodness, my life was negative before"* —because now you're so aware of the negative things. Because you're being so positive, the negative just seems huge Say you're at 75% negative and at 25% positive and you radically shift it around so you're 75% positive and you're 25% negative—guess what? —that 25% negative was always in your life, but you were so busy being negative that you didn't acknowledge it. Now that you're positive, you have the skills and the knowing how to deal with the *"Hello!"*, *"Hello!"*, *"Hello!"* You now know how to re-qualify your energy. Now the negative is down to 15%. Then eventually it's at 10%.

So the more positive you get, the more constructive you get in your life, it's going to seem like, *"Goodness, I was happier not having the negative in my life,"* but it was always there. You were just numb to it. You were being numb to those things in your life. They were always there. Now you are aware that you want to fix them, and that you have the opportunity to re-qualify them. You have the choice and the accountability to re-qualify that negative energy with love, forgiveness, gratitude and understanding. Find the opportunity and flip the negative to positive! It is ALL good.

Why do I say gratitude? I am grateful for every opportunity in my day that I can pour love, blessings, forgiveness, mercy, understanding, and patience into… no matter the appearance. Only perfection is eternal… everything else is like shifting sand on the ocean shore …constantly changing.

By choosing to be positive, by choosing to be in a place of love, loving myself, loving other people, what happens then is, when somebody comes back to you with that "hello!" message, you know

Life ABSOLUTES

the reason for it. You take that positive knowledge that you learn, and you will incorporate it into your life. What happens is that what was negative at one time is now positive. Or you say, *"That is their choice, Bless them, Forgive them, Assist them."* Have compassion. You will gain the mastery of knowing what to say and not say, what actions to have and not have.

Sometimes the negativity you feel is the energy left behind by others in the area. It is like the "Pigpen" cloud. Do not own it. Be grateful you are happy and move on!

So, on a pie chart—you're at 75% positive energy. You take that and say, *"Hello!"* all of a sudden—this is really great—you can go up to 80% positive energy. Because you absorb back into your life that energy you put out and you make it positive. Find the value in it. Find the wisdom in it. Find the compassion, the love, the forgiveness in it. Or just say, *"That's their choice"* or *"that is not my negative energy. I am experiencing—'Pig Pen'."* Image 22

You might have people in your life who are just going to be angry no matter what. They're going to be mad, they're going to hate the world, and they choose to stay there. And they're going to want to come into your world. And the people who have been pulling all that

Accountability

wonderful positive energy off of you come to you with the negative stuff; they're going to fight really hard to stay in your world. Because negative energy cannot exist by itself; it has to feed off positive energy. It has to feed off of positive energy! So they're going to fight really hard to push your buttons. They're going to figure out what really gets to you. We all know those kinds of people. And you say, *"Why do I do that every time I see that person? I just lose it!"*—because they know what buttons to push, because they want your energy. Until you stop allowing them to push your buttons, they're going to stay in your world. When they can't push your buttons anymore, they go bye-bye. They go find somebody else. They fall by the wayside.

Image 23

Life ABSOLUTES

Another really exciting thing that happens is that the negative person who was fighting so hard to be negative, even though you kept being positive, feels your energy. That person takes it in. They come and join your world, because you've made a positive influence on them. By constantly being compassionate and forgiving and uplifting, and pointing out the positive things that they have in their life and helping them find the positive things in their life, you became that person who changed their perception. Your constant positive energy defused their negativity and showed them how much better it feels to be positive. Notice I said they became positive from your example. Avoid wanting to go out and convert people. Did you want to be forced to change? Set the example and your life energy will lift them up! **This is a wonderful Double Blessing!**

Some people might leave your life; some people might be joining the ride with you to be positive. To have abundance in your health, in your relationships, in your job, in your finances—whatever you call success in your life—comes from being positive, because Divine Love (Positive energy) is unlimited abundance that constantly expands the more it is used.

TRUTH: You put something negative out? Well, it has to come back as something negative. The Law is the Law. And the way that it comes back to you could be through a person, it could be through a condition, it could be through a thing, it has to come back to you. And so when that negative thing comes back, this is what you do: You say, *"Hello! I recognize you! My human created you! When my human was being on a terror last week, deciding to be angry and mad and frustrated and depressed, it created you, so you have come back to me."*

It has to come back to you. So when something that I perceive is negative comes back into my world I say, *"All right. Hello. I'm going to make you positive because I can do that,"* and I find the positive thing in that situation. I say, *"Hello! I am going to acknowledge that my human created you or you are just someone else's negative energy lurking behind—the Pig Pen cloud. And now I'm going to deal with you. And I'm going to be happy that you came*

Accountability

back and now I can move on or say you're not mine and I am still happy." Perhaps that means you apologize to somebody. Handle it. So what happened to your world is you had that 5% negative energy. Every time you say 'Hello,' you're raising the positive number up and dissolving the negative. You're giving yourself better odds of having really great blessings happening in your life. Your relationships get getter. Your finances get better. Your health gets better. Your energy gets better. Your career gets better. Everything that you're pursuing in your life gets better because that's the way energy works. Perhaps you're arguing right now. That is your EGO knowing it is going down! It has been busted for the destroyer that it is.

TRUTH: Your world is a whole in a part of the whole universe. Your choices affect all life. Your energy is like the pebble that is tossed into the lake and makes the ripple. Your energy ripples the whole world including your own.

Image24

You are raising or lowering the whole rate of vibration in the world. That is accountability. Energy is tied together. So your choices are not just about you, they are about life. So please be accountable!

Life ABSOLUTES

TRUTHS RECAP: $[(e^E)\ T]A = Outcome$

- I am creating New Positive habits.
- When the appearance of a negative comes into my world I say, *"Hello! My human created you."* I am going to find the lesson, the blessing or the realization that I can just let it go and raise my rate of vibration even higher in my world. I am cleaning up my world. Victory Dance!!!
- I am <u>accountable</u> to the whole world for my emotionally driven thoughts and actions! Every single one of them. My choice affects the rate of vibration of the whole world!!!

Now that my life is becoming better, GREAT, AWESOME!!! How do I become successful in life? I am happy but not focused. *"HOW do I know what to do with my life?"* you ask.

That's the million-dollar question in the world, isn't it? What do I want? What do I want? Well, you want what's going to make you happy. But what is really going to make you happy? Perhaps you chased the dollar; that didn't seem to work. You chased the relationship; that didn't seem to work. You chased the job; that didn't seem to work. So what am I supposed to be going after?

Read the next chapter—Your Purpose in Life. You are in for a treat!

"I couldn't have made those changes without you!!!! When I say you're my angel, I'm being quite serious. If I hadn't found you (and I do believe I was guided to you), I would still be wondering what to do with my life! Now, I know and have the courage to follow my dreams and won't quit until they come true!!! I really can't thank you enough!!!!!!" -Christina Rivers-Los Angeles, CA Actress

CHAPTER 8

YOUR PURPOSE IN LIFE

YOUR LIFE'S BLUEPRINT

Now that you understand the power of your emotions, thoughts and actions plus, your focus/attention and how to re-qualify your life energy...

Here's THE question: What is YOUR purpose in life? Do you know what your purpose in life is? So many people think that it is an intangible, that it's a mystical question and you can never figure out the answer. I'm here to tell you, it's a very simple answer. Anybody know what your purpose in life is? Does anybody have an idea? Do you have an idea?

This is really going to help you know how to get up every day and be positive. The answer is the same for every single person in the world.

Stop reading and write down your answer on a piece of paper. Go ahead write. For those having resistance that is your EGO making excuses to sabotage you. Every time you ignore the EGO it gets weaker and weaker and YOU gain more mastery! More positive energy. More Successes. More MASTERY! GO AHEAD. The time is NOW. Write before you move ahead ☺.

"Seek ye first the kingdom of heaven and all else will be added unto you." -The Bible

TRUTH: What is my purpose in life? *To love myself and others which means you love the source of all life.*

Got it? You got it all the way back at the beginning of this information. You're staying true to that energy which flows through the universe—that which is love. The only way that you will be happy as an individual is to love yourself and to give love to other

67

Life ABSOLUTES

people. And once again, it's not romantic love. I'm talking about being compassionate, forgiving, grateful, patient, giving, inspiring, happy, joyful...love in action.

The purpose in life is love. **Your purpose in life is love!** I know, how truly simple. The EGO does not want it to be that simple...then it does not have a job. There is nothing to be confused about, nothing to cause chaos, nothing to worry about, nothing to fear, doubt, be guilty about, feel worthless about, stress about...NOTHING for the EGO to do. YES!!! Bye-bye EGO.

Live in the state of love. What does that do? Living in the state of love triggers the action of helping others. So the careers that we choose enable us to help other people. That's why we go out and have careers.

All we want is love...*go ahead and sing along...*

All we want is love. Absolutely. That is it! In the universe there is only one cause and that is love. We live in a cause and effect world right now. Because we have cause and we have the end result which is that *outpicturing*. Right now, a lot of the *outpicturing* is destructive or it's negative. When you start living in the state of love, you only have cause, because you have "Love-Love". Like the saying, "Win-Win". So it all boils down to love.

When you're always doing something positive, you only have Love-Love, which is great. So that's the ultimate experience that we're seeking. That's why the human being has this drive every day for something better. Because what happens is when you're living in a state of love, what do you desire to do? You desire to uplift other people around you. When you're in that place, when you get all happy, don't you desire to go out and get all of your other friends happy with you? That's why we have careers, relationships, hobbies. They fulfill that desire and that passion to uplift other people. You're reaching out and touching people when you're doing your "job." You're sharing that compassion. You're sharing joy. You're sharing happiness, that elation. You're sharing knowledge. It's great! You're

Your Purpose in Life

in a state of giving, and that's what we love to do as masterful beings. When we give, the automatic thing that happens is—because it comes back—we receive. But you can't receive unless you give. So you're giving positive, you get to receive positive back. When you're giving negative—hey! I didn't write the rules—you get the negative back. These are universal laws. I didn't create them; I'm reminding you of them.

So, you desire to live in a state of love. So now you know what your purpose is. That's where the passion comes in. **I am finding those activities that allow me to be passionate.** So when you wake up in the morning, you remind yourself, *oh my goodness, this is why I love my "job,"* this person, this activity! So I suggest that you write down a little, one paragraph statement of why you love what you do in your life. What does it fulfill for you? What does your "job" fulfill for you on a daily basis? Keep it in your car. Put it on your dashboard. Put it at your desk. Put it in the most conspicuous place you can think of so you are reminded daily—perhaps hourly—what your purpose is. Put it on your mirror!

Remind yourself every day when you get up to stay in that positive energy that is going to bring you everything that you could possibly want. Get up every day knowing that every **emotion** that you have will be an **emotion** of love. Every thought that you have will be a kind thought, a compassionate thought, a generous thought, a giving thought, a caring thought, and a positive thought. And every *action*, then, will end up being the same. A loving *action*, a kind *action*, a thoughtful *action*, a compassionate *action*, one of humility. And humility doesn't mean that you don't think you're worthy. Humility means that you know that you're on this course and the only reason your life is as good as it is, is because you're on this course. The Law of Oneness—Love. The Causeless cause. That means the cause and effect cycle stops because your life becomes the expansion of the cause—Love! You are free from the wheel of limitations-discord.

I'm not saying to love the actions of somebody that you know are destructive. You have compassion for that person. When somebody is a murderer, I'm not asking you to love the act of murder. You're

Life ABSOLUTES

having compassion for that person because that person created murder, because they were the person that was down in that numbness. They were so far removed from love that they didn't have any reason to live. They were in so much pain, and that pain became so great that they basically couldn't feel anymore because it hurt too much to feel. They are experiencing lack of love —lack of positive emotions.

When people do violent acts, it's because what they really want is love. They want compassion. They want understanding. They want somebody to care. And I'm not talking about sympathy. You don't have sympathy for somebody, because sympathy actually is a negative emotion. You don't sympathize with somebody who got thrown in jail. It was their choice—they made a choice to be in jail; you don't sympathize with that. You can have compassion. Compassion is an understanding that that person requires some assistance on learning how to make better choices.

So every day you get up because you love what it is that you get to do in that day. Great things are going to happen for you. Really, really good things are going to happen for you. And it's really exciting, because you can find the most interesting things about which you never realized that you'd be happy. Example, I went to a client's business just to drop some things off and as I was getting ready to leave Jennifer, the sales person, comes out to talk to me briefly—*"How are you? Good to see you."* And we had a quick conversation, then I left and I got in my car, and it saved me from being in a car accident. I am now sitting in traffic. Am I saying, *"Oh this is just really horrible?"* NO, I don't think about that anymore. I think, *"Oh my goodness this is a good thing—I'm in traffic because it could have been me in that accident."* I am sitting here in traffic now thinking about all the positive things that I have in my life. I am so grateful. OK, I'm going to do this when I get home; I'm going to do that when I get home. I didn't have time to think about these things. So now I'm in traffic and I have time to think about these things. I now have time to really listen to that CD I really like. Normally, I arrive home in fifteen minutes and I never get to listen to the whole thing. Now I have 45 minutes, so that's a positive thing. I

Your Purpose in Life

now get to listen to my CD. I get to do my gratitude time. I get to acknowledge the blessings that are in my life!!!

Everything that you have a negative perception of can be turned into a positive. You're going to be able to find a positive outcome! What this does is it starts changing your behavior. Right now, some of you might have the behavior of liking to be negative. This is your comfort zone. It's familiar to you, so you stay there. I'm here to tell you that it takes discipline. It is going to take determination. I would love to take a magic wand and make everything perfect for you right now. You would be living this wonderfully glorious life. You'd never be required to deal with anything negative ever again. That would be really incredible. However, in reality—you would go out and make the destructive choices again until you learned the lessons.

You have the skills now to know, in every moment of every day, that you can make a choice that's guided by your emotions. And some of you are going to first learn that you have emotions. Some of you are first going to say, *"Oh my goodness, I'm having an emotion right now. Wow! That's what this is. I didn't even know that I was having emotions before."*

So for some of you, going forward, you're just going to start in the place of taking time to acknowledge every time you realize you're having a different emotion. You will want to do this until you are aware that you're having emotions. Otherwise, how will you know how you're qualifying your energy? You won't, because society has told us to be emotionless people, basically. We've been told that and been raised that way.

Emotions weren't created so we could have greeting cards. Emotions weren't created so we could have holidays. Those are things that we sometimes associate with emotions. Emotions are to help you in every moment of every day go wherever it is that your dream is, wherever you want to go with your dream. Remember the first emotion was LOVE. All the other ones were created to deal with the choices the human makes. Stay in the emotion of love and be the causeless cause. Love in action. This is the masterful way of life. The

Life ABSOLUTES

enlightened way which blesses the world, your family and yourself.

Our whole purpose in life is to love. So what is it you love to do in life? Write those things down for yourself Right NOW. Yes, right now. ☺ Dream big…it is YOUR destiny to be great! Write down as many ideas that pop into your head. Be Fearless!!! You will probably start crying tears of joy…your EGO will tell you it is fear. That EGO is such a deceiver. Go ahead write.

OK. Is there one choice that has a greater purpose in life for you than any of the other choices—or which one of your choices stands out the most? Say you could not do one of them for the rest of your life without being absolutely miserable…which one is it?

ANSWER: LOVE…OK, besides love?

OK, so how do you incorporate that in your everyday life?
AND THE OTHER OPTIONS that you love to do in life?

This one thing is most likely what you **should base your career** on—that passion. Now say you wrote down ideas that are based purely on gratification of the senses….that is your EGO again. Go back and be honest.

Me—I love to share with people how to be happy. Ever since I was a child, I felt people were meant to be truly happy. Why aren't people happy? I want people to know how to be happy, how to find that happiness we're all promised. I didn't understand as a child why people couldn't always be happy. And so my life has taken me on this journey from one thing to another that allowed me to share with people how you can be happy, how I can uplift people, how I can say positive things that are genuine to people on a daily basis.

Each one of you has something that resembles love that you want to share with mankind in one way, shape or form. There's something that you love to give because it just really excites you—inspires you.

You are excited when you're living it. You know, you can be tired,

Your Purpose in Life

and when you talk about it, your eyes light up, your body gets this tingling all over because that's what you're really, really, really passionate about. You have passion for "it." A skill, a talent and gift—YOUR purpose! What is it? Carpenter, lawyer, house wife, teacher, electrician, musician, plumber, banker, athlete, writer, parent...what is it?

Perhaps you're doing something in your life that you're not passionate about, ask yourself, "Is there a way that the passion can be rekindled?" Is this opportunity providing a means to an end that is positive?

Example: Is the opportunity paying your way through college, allowing you to save to start a business? Do not settle for less, however, BE HONEST, and BE accountable. **Perhaps you are where you are supposed to be for now.** Are you the one that requires an attitude adjustment? Should you be more grateful and understanding? Should the answer become 'no,' then it's time to move on. Just because you're in one place with your life at one time in your life, doesn't mean you can't move on to another place. Sometimes you're in a place because the knowledge that you gained from being there creates an opportunity to go to the next place where you're supposed to be. You gain knowledge in life and keep going forward and doing things about which you are passionate.

Back when I was a baton teacher, I woke up one day and said, *"Oh, this is so not what I want to do anymore!"* And I moved on. However, those skills and that knowledge that I learned, I've used throughout my life. So it wasn't a waste of time; it was very, very valuable and it moved me on to be able to do other things. So life is constantly giving you knowledge when you acknowledge it.

Replace the word "job" with activity. That is why the word "job" is in "italics" early in this book. The activity that you do for 40 hours a week, give or take, is what allows you to be love in action, passion in action, creativity in action, gratitude, compassion, forgiveness, giving in action. The activity that allows your life energy to flow abundantly out to all life, raising it up, creating more joy, more

Life ABSOLUTES

abundance, better health and more freedom. This is EXCITING and liberating! Just by being love in action you personally are improving the whole world including your own. Well done! Of course everything now becomes an activity. Joy Of Being: J.O.B.

Have fun with this process. **Perhaps you will stay where you are while you are creating the opportunity for you to move into your new activity in life.** Always keep yourself in the place of loving yourself and life around you.

Here are the words to a wonderful song. It is called, *"I Choose Love".*

I can see laughter, or I can see tears
I see a choice, love or fear
What do you choose?
I can see peace, or I can see war
I can see sunshine, or I can see a storm
What do you choose?

Now I choose to live with freedom flying
From my heart, where the light keeps shining
I choose to feel the whole world crying
For the strength that we can rise above
I choose Love
I choose Love

I can see sharing, or I can see greed
I can see caring, or poverty
What do you choose?
I can see gardens, or I can see bombs
I can see life, or death

Coming on strong
What do you see?

Your Purpose in Life

Now I choose…

I see healing, the darkness dying
I see us dawning, as one world united
What do you choose?
Love or fear
Oh, we choose

Now I choose to live with freedom flying
From my heart, where the light keeps shining
I choose to feel the whole world crying
I choose to feel one voice rising
I choose to feel us all united
In the strength that we can rise above
I choose Love
I choose Love
Oh, I choose Love

Permission granted by Shawn Gallaway to share his song's words. You can buy his powerful CD called, *"I Choose Love"* @ www.ShawnGallaway.com

Perhaps the "gift," "skill" you have does not seem to have a career created around it. Well, neither did the inventor of the computer, the car, and the airplane. It is more than OK to be self-employed as long as you stay motivated and stay willing to learn and you can be happy with the consequences of your choices. Keep fear out of the equation.

TRUTHS RECAP: $[(e^E)\ T]A = Outcome$

- My purpose in life is to be love in action.
- My career is an activity that allows me to express love and my passion in action.
- My relationships, my career, my health are all ways for me to express love in action.
- I am the law of oneness when I am love in action.

Life ABSOLUTES

SMILE

*A Smile costs nothing, but gives much
It enriches those who receive, without making poorer those who give*

It takes but a moment, but the memory of it sometimes lasts forever

*None is so rich or mighty that he can get along without it,
and none is so poor, but that he can be made rich by it*

*A Smile creates happiness in the home, fosters goodwill in business,
and is the countersign of friendship*

*It brings rest to the weary, cheer to the discouraged, sunshine to the
sad, and it is nature's best antidote for trouble.*

*Yet it cannot be bought, begged, borrowed, or stolen,
for it is something that is of no value to anyone, until it is given away*

*Some people are too tired to give you a smile;
Give them one of yours, as none needs a smile so much as he who
has no more to give.* -Author unknown

Now that you understand the power of your emotions, thoughts and actions plus, your focus/attention and you know what your Purpose in Life is—you are ready to discover where you live. That's right where are you living in your activity of life?

Where Are You Living

CHAPTER 9

WHERE ARE YOU LIVING?

THE THREE CITIES

This is your world. It now looks like an airplane—like a three-year-old's airplane. Your life is really going well. And when you fly an airplane, you put it on a course and it can have these little variances and still get you to where you want to be. Those little variances are those growth points in your life—those knowledge-gaining moments that you have in your life—AH*HA moments. And you require those. That's what's called challenge/opportunity in life. Say, we didn't want to be better; we would be great big adults still in diapers and sucking on pacifiers. We have a desire to evolve into smarter, more talented, enlightened, awakened—whatever it is—individuals. We have that innate desire to expand our life's perfections—greater mastery! Image 25

You are in your airplane. And this is the flying zone of success—the State of Success. That's that energy that's pure and perfect, and it's unobstructed by negative thoughts, negative actions, negative emotions. And you're in that power of passion and confidence and being happy and being grateful. You're flying along

Image 26

Life ABSOLUTES

(on your plane), and you're flowing in the direction to greater abundance, which is a positive place. This is all a positive journey and it is a sign of success because you're doing what you like to do every day and things are going how you want them to go, and you keep getting better, keep getting better, you're being successful at that moment. You are being grateful. So, you're being successful, you're going along and life is going great, and you have your friends in your airplane. One day something disastrous in "appearance" happens and you become really upset. You become really angry. You become really frustrated.

We'll go back to the college example—you were going to college. Life was going along, and things were going great, and that's when you hit that bump in the road—turbulence—challenge/opportunity. You had your friends in your airplane, and that's when the horrible day happened, when you were going for your teaching certificate. The world came to an end; it ganged up against you; and it was just the most horrible experience that could possibly happen. You failed the test. And you tell all your friends and you have this really great pity party for yourself. You party for a week, finding everything bad in the world. And what happens during that party is one of your friends says, *"You know what? There's an opening where I am working. You have all the skills for it. Why don't you work at my job? I know I can get you that job. It pays really well."* And let's say you make that choice to quit, because your friend says, *"I've got a great job for you. Why don't you come up here?"*

So you go there…
with your friend and you start selling xyz. You have money. You have a car. You have a house. **You have the "American Dream."** You have the perfect relationship. You're out selling xyz. *"Whew! I'm rockin!"*

Where Are You Living

TRUTH: You wake up one day. *"Hhhhh, my job is the pits!"* Something happened. You heard somebody say, "I just got my teaching certificate," and you say, "Oh yeah, that's what I would like to do!" You start talking to them, "Yeah, I remember that. Yeah, oh yeah, that's so cool. That's what I want to be." You wake up, and you're really unhappy, and in our society (it's been called a mid-life crisis). What I'm here to tell you is that mid-life crisis is starting to happen to people before they're 40—in their 20's even. And I'm thrilled about that! Should you choose to get out of a job you are unhappy with, somebody else can then take your job because they really love that job. Once, again, you it's up to you to get yourself out of it...move on! You know!?

So get out of that chair, you don't want it; let somebody who wants it have it. Because there is a "right" job for everybody out there, but there are too many people in the wrong jobs. So, let's make yourself happy and see what happens! Everybody else gets the job they love.

You know why your job is the pits? Because you're not following your passion anymore. You abandoned your passion, your dream. In appearance, you've got the American Dream. You have all the money you want. You have the perfect car. You have the perfect house. You have the perfect relationship. You have paid vacation time. Goodness! You're working with your friend, my goodness, what else could you possibly desire!? You're saving up for a yacht; why aren't you happy?

Because you desire to be able to be doing in life what you're passionate about. So what has happened is you're living in the **City of Settle for Less.** You are living a lie.

TRUTH: You settled. *"I'll go after the dollar." "The easy way out." "The Quick Fix."* You did not see the failing of the test as an opportunity.

What happens when you stay in the "City of Settle for Less" too long? The money starts going by the wayside because you don't like coming to work anymore.   Your relationships start breaking down

Life ABSOLUTES

because you're not happy anymore. Your partner's saying, *"You used to be so happy. What's troubling you?"*

You went after the money. The money doesn't make you happy  anymore. The car doesn't make you happy anymore. Working with your friend doesn't make you happy anymore—your friend's so doggone happy every day because your friend is really, really doing what he loves to do, but you're not really happy and no one can understand why you're not happy anymore. Image 28

"I don't know. I'm just not happy. It's hard to get out of bed. I don't like my job." The car starts breaking down, and all these things start happening in your life, it starts falling apart because you have this negative energy going out and now it is coming into your world, and your world starts decaying. You find yourself complaining all the time. You get home at the end of the day and you're exhausted, because you haven't done what you enjoy. You're in a constant state of focusing on the negative. And the negative drains the energy right out of you. So you do not enjoy your new car; you do not enjoy the money that you have, you now want to come home, click on the TV and sit there like a lump on the sofa. You don't have energy to do those things that you love to do, the things that you did at one time, because the negative energy that you put out about your job has sucked the life right out of you. So this job and all that money and that car don't mean anything because it's all materialistic. It doesn't fulfill what you want to be fulfilled inside of you…you start spending more than you make, cheating or partying for a quick fix.

TRUTH: You are living in the "City of Settle for Less."

So what happens next is you have the freedom of choice. You can get back in your airplane, study for the test, fulfilling what you desire

Where Are You Living

to do, fuel up your airplane with passion and intense determination and get back in the "State of Success."

You aren't happy here settling for less, whatever it might be. It might be a relationship, it might be the city you're living in, whatever it may be, you are settling and there's something out there you really want in your life and you've given up on it for awhile, you are in the City of Settle for Less or worse.

At any time, you can get back in your airplane. You can put a smile on your face. Your friends are not supportive, they're saying, *"Oh my goodness, I can't believe you're going to be a teacher. It's such a stupid idea, blah blah blah blah,"* then don't let those people get back in your airplane with you because they're destructive. They're negative. They're holding you back. They're stealing your dream from you. You don't desire those kinds of friends in your life, because they're not a friend. They're distracting you from flying the plane and you don't want to crash. You want to stay on course.

People say, *"You know what? When I started being positive I lost all my friends."* Well, then they weren't your friends to begin with! Those people were helping you stay in the negative, helping you stay in that lack, helping you stay in that despair, helping you stay in that misery. They were helping you with that. Is that a real friend?

So you get back in your plane and what happens is you find somebody who is really supportive of you and is always going to be supportive of you, and they're the "flagger" for you. Airplanes landed back in the day using a flagger on the ground, a kind of traffic controller. Even enlightened people have "flaggers."

What happens sometimes is we tell everybody what our passions and dreams are and some people, because they're miserable, don't want you to have your dream. They are the **"Dream Stealers."** Or, perhaps you're in your airplane, and you're going to the City of success, and you hit another bump in the road while you're being interviewed for a teaching position. There's big turbulence. Huge bump in the road. You talk to your flagger person and you don't

81

Life ABSOLUTES

want to believe them. You don't want to see the positive in it, and you just say, *"I'm fed up with this. I can go back to my job. I can have the money. It's easy."* You decide to stay in the "City of Settle for Less" for too long, your airplane takes a nosedive into this city where everything is all boarded up. The windows are boarded up. There's not even a horse at the hitching post. You're in an abandoned ghost town. This is the **"City of Abandoned Dreams."**

TRUTH: The City of Abandoned Dreams is where the people who have pity parties live. City of Abandoned Dreams is where you say, *"You know what? I'm not good enough. I'm a loser. I'm a failure. The world hates me. It's my parents' fault. It's my mom's fault. It's my dog's fault. It's my ex-wife's fault. It's my boyfriend's fault. It's my boss's problem that I got fired. It's my girlfriend's problem that I got fired. It's the government's problem that I'm unemployed. It's unemployment's problem that I am unemployed. It's my teacher's ... It's the ant on the ground's problem! It's the whole world's fault; it's not my fault. This is God's big Joke."*

This is where the parties are rocking. There's a party every single day, and the kind of party that I'm talking about is a pity party. That's where the "blamer" people hang out—The City of Abandoned Dreams, because every day, their life energy is spent on explaining to the world, and justifying to the world why they didn't get their teaching certificate. *"It was that teacher, Mr. Smith! My parents are horrible people!"*

Whatever it is, you sit down and circle around your little pow-wow, and you do your best to validate, *"Why, your life stinks just like my life! Hey! We've got something in common, our lives stink together!"* Image 29

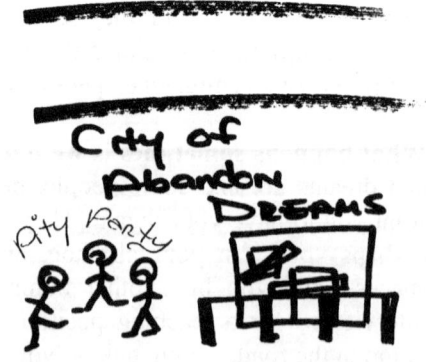

Wow! That's really something to celebrate. This

Where Are You Living

is true. You do! You come down here and you get together on a regular basis and talk about how the world stinks and how it's unfair, and your childhood was horrible, and this and that and the other thing, and it's everybody's fault but your own.

TRUTH: It's all an excuse. It's an excuse; this program is about accountability. You are accountable for your actions. Should you choose to do something destructive, then you are accountable for that outcome. When you choose to do something positive, then you're more than happy to be accountable. The pity party is the syndrome of *"I won't be accountable for the garbage that I created in my life,"* so you get your so-called friends, you sit around and complain about the world and supposedly feel better about yourself. This is a perfect example of the "quick fix" —you feel better while you are complaining—then later you feel even worse. It's the spiral. Every time you have a pity party, you're going further and further down that spiral. Further and further down in your rate of vibration, further away from love!

Those are the people who live in the "City of Abandon Dreams." They're blaming the whole world for why they didn't succeed and go after whatever passion it is that they have in life. You want success in your health, in your relationships, in your job, in your finances, whatever it is. Should you give up on them and tell yourself you can't have it because it's somebody else's fault or better yet YOUR fault? Poor me... you're in the City of Abandoned Dreams!

And I'm here with good news; you can get out of the City of Abandoned Dreams just like that. (Snap your fingers) You can get focused, charged up with positive emotions, make a plan of action...that looks like a ladder...climb up into your airplane. You can fuel it up with your passion (positive emotions) and get back up here in the State of

Life ABSOLUTES

Success and go upward—and leave the pity party people behind.

Do not take them with you. The last thing you want to do is tell all the people around you what you're going to do with your life. *"I have this new revelation; I'm going to change my life."* The "party" people are going to be the people that'll talk you out of it in a New York second.

You're all excited and focused. You're fueled up. Your plane's ready to go. It's on the runway and the next thing you know, they've pulled the plug out of your fuel tank and your fuel is spilling out onto the ground. They've just drained it right out of you, just like that, because they don't want you to go and have your success, because then you're not there to have the pity party with them. Until they have sucked you dry—taken all your energy—they want you there. Remember, negative requires life energy to exist. They are running out and want YOURS!!! Sounds like a bad horror film.

Don't tell those people what you're going to do. Just get on your plane and go towards where you want to be, and here in the City of Success you have somebody that you can trust, someone who's positive and a support system for you. When you call up and say, *"Man, my day bit the big one!"* they say, *"All right. Let's talk about it. Let's find the positive in it because you know what happens when you're negative."*

Back to your friend, your friend that is happy because they are living their dream, they're doing what they love to do. Perhaps they are your flagger. In reality they might be living their dream. Let them in your airplane!!! Free boarding pass. They don't "party" in the pity party. They don't encourage you go out and get bombed out of your mind. They encourage you to sit down and figure out what the positive thing is out of that lesson—what the "hello" was, so that you keep staying focused on where you want to go.

Find yourself a flagger. Your flagger could be a parent, a teacher, a spiritual leader, a friend or a relative. I am a flagger for a lot of clients all year round.

Where Are You Living

"Karen LaVoie is a positive, high-energy, talented person ...she is unstoppable."
-Cynthia Kersey,
Author of *'Unstoppable'* and many other books

Image 31

TRUTH: At any time, you can leave the City of Abandoned Dreams. Get back in your airplane soar up! It's all about choice. Focus on what you desire. Focus on what **you** desire. **At any time you can make the choice to find the positive,** and come out of the

Life ABSOLUTES

City of Abandon Dreams, back up into your airplane, and be in the state, in the mind set and focus of success and still have it. You can choose any moment in any day to make that happen in your life!

Make choices that uplift and serve mankind.

What happened yesterday has no effect on right here, right now unless you choose for it to have an effect. Right here, right now, choosing to be positive, choosing to have compassion, choosing to have love is going to create the positive tomorrow that you're seeking. Looking in the past and digging up all the garbage and staying in that and wallowing in it only creates in the "now" more negative. So you keep re-creating what's been in the past. That's why people say, *"Why does this keep happening to me? UGH! It's like the tenth time now!"*

Because you keep doing the same thing over and over again, that's why! You know, you've created the formula for that bad thing to keep happening in your life. You keep following the same formula. Stop it! You can stop that same old pattern and create a positive pattern to replace it. You're watching reruns of your life—STOP. Make a new series that is joyful and masterful.

Certainly, you go into your past and you can do the, *"Please forgive me. I apologize. Can I make this better?"* Don't go back and go, *"Oh, I am such a screw up,"* because that doesn't help you right now. All that does is puts you back in the place of being negative. You're not a screw up. Guess what? We're all on this journey learning how to be better people. You **now** have a formula, your instruction manual that allows you to go forward and make more positive choices to get these dreams that you want, to fulfill that passion, to live with that passion in your life every day. So right here, right now you say, *"Yes! OK! Right here, right now I'm going to choose to be positive"*. The second that one of those little bumps in the road happens say, *"That's right, oh, Hello! Hello! I'm going to be positive again. Hello! Hello! Hello! Hello, can you hear me now? All right."* So you're going to start sounding like a Verizon commercial, and that's OK, because the more you say hello, the

Where Are You Living

more you know that you're changing the habits of your life. You're plucking out the negative in your life by being love in action!!!

Notice when you have people in your airplane who just want to be negative, you know; those people who were around your circle earlier in the book?

Because we're such positive people, sometimes, it is necessary to kick them off the airplane and we give them a parachute, and we wish them all the best. Image 32

We don't wish them any harm; we don't hate them or anything. We wish them the best; we have compassion for them. Guess what? It doesn't work in my life anymore. I'm moving on. I'm choosing to have positive people around me. It doesn't mean you don't reach out to people and give love to them, give compassion, give support, do charity, give out to the community —don't bury yourself in those relationships. ***Be in the world but not of it.***

In life we have what's called challenge. And that challenge is what motivates us to learn, to gain knowledge. We do not require road blocks. We do not have to have these humungous road blocks, those things that absolutely tear us apart. The second that you stop doing all the negative stuff, all those big hurdles start going away. And you just get what's called—OPPORTUNITY. And that is good. You're at this place in your life; you want more knowledge. And that opportunity is good, because it forces you to keep expanding—more

Life ABSOLUTES

confidence, more knowledge, more wisdom, and more mastery, that's what YOU want. Otherwise you become stagnant, you grow old, you "die" and then you pass on. And you didn't really fulfill what it was you were supposed to fulfill.

You say to yourself or your friendly flagger, *"Hello! What's the message here? What's the knowledge to be gained in this situation? What's the opportunity that I can create from this?"* That's what that friend helps you do. Those are the kinds of friends you want in your world. You don't want the pity party, dream stealer people in your world. And you are going to have people that fall by the wayside, once again: they weren't your friends to begin with when they do not choose to join you in this upward climb.

Knowing all of this, you can live in the State of Success and the City of Success, the place of being happy, of having good health, of having abundance, of having those relationships that you desire. And when I say 'success,' I'm not necessarily talking about money. I'm talking about that balance in your life that gives you peace and joy every day. You get up and you feel fulfilled at the end of every day. The City of Success is that which represents each goal you achieve in life. Each small, medium and large goal you achieve in life. ALWAYS acknowledge the goals achieved, no matter how minute.

TRUTH: Without minute goals being achieved, you do not achieve the larger goals! Think about that. Be in Gratitude all day long.

There's a question that I ask myself that I want you to hear for the positive question that it is. When they hear it, some people say, *"That is so morbid,"* it's actually a very, very positive question. I ask myself, *"Were I to 'make the change—cross over today,' have I done what truly makes me happy in my life? Have I done what truly makes me happy in life?"* When I get a "no" answer, I ask myself why? That is the next thing on my agenda to change in my life—time is very precious. Life is very precious. To hang out in the City of Settle for Less and say, *"Oh, I'll do it when this gets done. I'll do it when the kids leave home. I'll do it when I get that debt paid off."* You know what? Life is what allows you to be alive—respect it, be

Where Are You Living

grateful for it and do not take it for granted! You don't know that "some day" is ever going to come. And I don't mean that to sound morbid; that's the reality of it. You have a dream, you have a passion, you act on it today—no regrets. This is my opinion. Go out and find what truly makes you happy, and do what truly makes you happy, incorporate it in your life, and start making it a reality in your life! Once again serving a higher purpose—Love in Action.

Then you'll always be in a State of Success. And you might have 20 or 30 or maybe only 1 City of Success. Those are goals in your life that are really going to keep you going, fulfilling the dreams that you're passionate about!

So you get back in your airplane, you're all fueled up because that's your passion, and that passion is a fuel that goes into your airplane. And over here in your City of Success you have your flagger so when you say, *"Omigosh, today was just like a living hell!"* The flagger says, *"OK, and your point is? What did you learn from it? What did you do that made it a living hell? Don't do it again. Hello!"*

You know, it really is that simple: whatever made it a living hell, don't do it again. You obviously didn't like the results of that. You flunked your test, why did you flunk your test? Maybe you didn't study enough. Or is it because emotions that you had and thoughts that you had and actions that you had caused you to flunk the test? So the person that's the bearer of the bad news isn't the problem. It's the choices that you made that caused the end result in

Life ABSOLUTES

your life. When your relationship's not working, what were the emotional choices and the thoughts and the actions that you took to make that relationship come to that place? Go back to focusing on all the positive things, and say it doesn't work after focusing on all the positive things, then it's possible it's time to move on. Image 33

The same with the job that you're in: It served its purpose. It served the purpose in your life to open up another door of opportunity. I didn't make this up—the one door has to be closed before the other one can open. I know that you have heard that before. It's the truth. Maybe you'll be that school teacher for 10 years and the next thing you know you're thinking, *"I don't like being a school teacher for second grade anymore. I want to be a professor."*

Well, that was a stepping stone to being the professor. You go back to school, you get the degrees that you require, and you become the professor. Now you have the knowledge, and the wisdom, the mastery and confidence, and the skill set to move on and be a professor.

Life's journey gives you confidence. The more positive choices that you make, the more confidence you gain. I'll say that again. The more positive choices you make the more confidence you gain. The more positive choices that you make, the more knowledge you have gained. Knowledge is experience. You know something when you've experienced it. Otherwise it's learned. You're taking the word of somebody else that this is the truth. And I'm here to tell you sometimes the "truth" is tainted by somebody else's negative opinion.

When somebody gives you advice—get a college education; get a job that pays really well—maybe that isn't your answer in life. Maybe that isn't what makes you happy. Maybe that's what would make them happy. Reality: Seek what's going to make you happy long term.

TRUTH: I know a person who's a millionaire who never made it past the seventh grade. I'm not advocating dropping out of school,

Where Are You Living

however I'm saying everybody has his or her path to take to find happiness—to nurture his or her success. College is not the answer for everybody. Trade school is not the answer for everybody.

Being self-employed is not the answer for everybody. Being a pro athlete is not the answer for everybody. Not everybody in the world wants to be a carpenter. Not everybody in the world wants to be a garbage person. Not everybody in the world wants to be—you fill in the blank. We all have our own dream. So when people give you advice, decide whether it has validity or not for YOU. You know? *"Don't do this." "Ooh, well, why?" "Don't put your hand on a hot stove"*—I tell you, that has validity…ouch. I think we've all checked that out at least once in life to know it has validity, and it's a really good knowing to have. But sometimes advice that people give us comes from a place of fear. They sat down and had a pity party for themselves. So that's why they're saying, *"Don't be a school teacher. That's so hard to do. It's really, really hard."* That's their reality, not yours.

Go out and get advice from people who already are successful in what it is you would like to accomplish. Ask them, *"How did you become successful in this?"* Usually their advice is pretty good, because they know all of the positive ways to get there. Don't ask them to list all of the bad things that happened along the way, because then you've planted those little seeds in your mind. Ask them, *"What are all the positive things that happened for you to get here?"* Tell me about all the positive things because then, what are you doing? YOU know the answer? Yes! You're focusing on the positive.

People like to be helpful and say, *"You know what, if you want to do such and such, don't do this. Don't do this. Don't do this. Don't do this. Don't do this."* The person may say, *"Oh, there are all these things I can't do."* And it stops them in their tracks. I know that we mean to be helpful, but sometimes when we overload people with all the things you're not supposed to do, they never get started because it seems so overwhelming! That emotion that we have is overwhelming. *"It's too overwhelming because there's so much that I*

Life ABSOLUTES

can't do and I'm supposed to be afraid of and be aware of—FEAR, why should I even start? Goodness! Geez, I'm buried in 3,000 pounds of all this stuff I'm supposed to be afraid of!"

TRUTH: Success—it's about making choices, right here, right now, in the moment, because that creates tomorrow, and the next tomorrow and the next tomorrow —thus the saying, "Live in the NOW." Make the NOW Positive! Positive emotions, positive thoughts, positive actions create the positive OUTCOME. I am excited!!! Are you excited? I thought so. Yes, AWESOME!

TRUTHS RECAP: $[(e^E)\ T]A = Outcome$

- I choose to live in the State of Success and the Cities of Success.
- "Pity Parties" are destructive.
- I have a flagger friend to call when I am tempted to overlook the positive in the so-called negative situations that appear in my world.
- My success is up to me. Sure others are there on the journey assisting me. However, ultimately I make the decision in every moment of every day to be positive no matter what the visible world (appearance world) shows me.
- When the desire is great enough the solution appears.
- I am in this world but not of it.

CHAPTER 10

TIMELINE

OPPOSITE WORLDS

In life we're looking for choices that fulfill us, that make us happy. When we're not finding those choices that fulfill us and make us happy, we get angry, and we get sad, and we get lonely, and we have fear, and we have doubt because of our perception that we are not fulfilling our purpose in life. It is selfish to not fulfill our purpose in life. You heard me right. SELFISH. Everyone including you has a gift and/or gifts to share with the world and when you do not fulfill your purpose you are not sharing those gifts, thus, leaving the rest of mankind to go "without."

What happens is that in a 24-hour day you want to accomplish a certain number of things in your life. You get up in the morning, you're really, really positive, *"Yes! I'm being positive! I'm excited! I'm positive about my day! I'm going to go and do this and this. And this is great! I feel good!"*

And you're cruising along, life is going good, and all of a sudden you hit a bump in the road. And the human intellect/EGO wants to say, *"This is unfair; I don't deserve this...NAH NAH NAH NAH NAH NAH NAH."* In reality, this is your "Hello!" moment. It could be left behind negative energy from someone else ("Pig Pen") that you are going to ignore, or it could be an opportunity for you to gain knowledge so that you can go forward and achieve what you want to achieve. The fact is the situation is positive, figure out why it is

Life ABSOLUTES

positive, so you can then gain greater wisdom. Mastery by the way is the actual application of wisdom on a moment to moment basis... walking the walk.

We have "the bumps in the road" as we go through life. Otherwise, we'd probably still be in kindergarten or pre-school. The bump in the road is learning your ABCs. The next bump in the road is learning two plus two equals four. The next bump is learning A plus B equals B plus A. OK? It's learning those lessons in life. It's gaining that knowledge so at some point in time you say, *"Oh, wow that's why I learned this; it helped me get to this important place."* That bump in the road could appear as the frustrated customer or it could be something that happens in your life. You've flunked the test that you were taking to become a teacher.

I'm here to share with you that little bump in the road has a message for you. And that message is that there's still some negative energy hanging around. You as an individual are being all positive now but, guess what? There's still some of that negative energy—we've got 24% of that negative energy still hanging out in the universe, and it comes back, right? That negative energy comes back to you in one way, shape or form. Maybe you walked into some else's negative energy. It could be a person, it could be a thing, it could be an incident, and when that comes back to you, the best thing that you can do is, you say, *"Hello! I recognize you. My human created you. At some point in time, my human created you. My human attracted you with my negative energy to come into my life and now it's being delivered back or I have my attention on you."*

What do you do when that negative comes back to you? Look for the message. What's the lesson that you can learn from this person, from this situation, from whatever it is that happened? This can easily be valid or it could be, *OK, they're entitled to their opinion*, or it opens up a dialogue or discussion so that you learn. You have knowledge gained from that experience. It is an opportunity for expanding yourself. Because maybe when you flunked that test there was something on there that you really, really should have known, you should have studied harder so that when you eventually did get hired

Timeline

to do whatever it is, that knowledge would come in handy one day. You don't know what day it is, you want to take that test over again, and really apply yourself, and really be open to the information you have been requested to learn so it can become knowledge, wisdom and mastery.

Image 35

TRUTH: In reality this bump in the road is actually a growth experience and you're gaining knowledge, because learned information is learned information. Learned information can turn into knowing—knowledge is a knowing. I know it. I know that this is true for me. I know how this works in my life. So that bump in the road, actually, that "hello" is an important thing in your life. It's allowing you to change this into a positive, into something constructive in your life. The result is that whoever it was, or whatever situation it was that brought it to you has now been transformed. You've uplifted somebody! You've helped somebody have a better life or you've created a better situation by finding a positive reason for this happening and gaining the knowledge and

Life ABSOLUTES

taking that as a growth experience. You've improved whatever the situation is. Perhaps the lesson is as simple as, it was negative energy left behind by others.

Remember, the Princess Diana and J.F.K. example—do not own the negative energy of others. Bless it and move on.

You keep going through your day, you might get a little bump you say, *"OK, another 'hello'"*—I've had days when I've had 24 "hellos" in my life. Wow! OK! This is good, because the more I get through, the sooner I get to 12%. You get through your day in eight hours and you've accomplished a lot of what you wanted to do. You go home and you are energized! You feel great—you accomplish more and go to bed with a happy smile in your heart and sleep peacefully and soundly. You wake up refreshed and excited about the new day!!! You are now a living breathing sun presence of love in action…a smiling heart! Image 36

Timeline

Now, when you choose to stay in the negative when you hit that bump in the road, it becomes a huge wall. You shut down, and you spend the rest of the day there. And then you throw yourself a pity party. *"It is not my fault that I flunked that test! That teacher did not give me those questions. Had the teacher talked about it in class, I would have known that stuff. It's not my fault. That teacher is such a loser and just doesn't like me. That's how come I flunked. It's not my fault; my roommate was up all night so I couldn't sleep and that's how come I didn't pass my test."*

You start blaming the whole world for the situation that came into your life, and you sit down and you have a pity party. You call up your friends who like to blame the rest of the world for all their problems and you get a pity party for a day, for a week, for a month, for the rest of your lifetime. *"It's everybody's fault that my life is terrible! I was doing so well. I was going to get my certificate as a teacher until that happened. It's that thing's fault. Or I am just a loser."* Then you stay there. And at the end of your eight-hour day,

Life ABSOLUTES

you've accomplished very little except creating more problems in your life. Image 37

You have more to deal with now, because when you happen to stay there for too long, you don't even get your teaching certificate. You quit your job or you end the relationship that maybe shouldn't have been ended because you didn't want to know what the growth or knowledge was in the opportunity. You want to see what that growth opportunity is supposed to be in every "so-called" negative appearance.

Well, whatever that was, it was the thing that was going to guarantee that you got the certificate. But because you wanted to focus on the negative, you never got your teaching certificate. And for the next 20 years of your life you complain about it. Complain, complain, complain, complain, complain, complain and complain. You never get to do what you really wanted to do because you weren't open to the knowledge you could gain. You didn't want to say, *"Hello! I recognize you. What is the value in this? What's the validity in this moment so that I can move forward and be a better individual, be the teacher that I really, really want to be?"*

TRUTH: Many times you just sit down and give up because it all seems too overwhelming and too difficult. You go home at the end of the day. You're exhausted. So all the obligations you have at the end of the day at home, you don't do them. Because you're tired. You're in a bad mood. You're having that conversation in your head of why the job doesn't work, and this doesn't work, and that doesn't work, and this person this, and that person that, and blah, blah, blah. You get nothing done for yourself, and you get up the next day and because you have all this negative energy, you're even more tired. You're less inspired.

Unless you do what I've talked about—choosing something positive to do, making a positive choice, finding out how to make this positive—you will end up in the pit. At any point in time, you can decide to make your life positive. The next thing you know, your day will end up fulfilled.   It won't be a waste of a day when you change

Timeline

your emotions, thoughts and attention.

I'm here to tell you, when you don't learn life's lessons—when you don't learn these lessons—they keep repeating. Remember the old saying, *"Why does this keep happening to me?"* Why? Because you didn't get it the first time. You didn't get it the second time. You didn't get it the third, the fifth, the hundredth. It's going to keep coming back to you until you get it! It will come back more negative, because you didn't get it and you made it more negative, it comes back again this time more negative.

I choose living in the life of the "positive world." Which life do you want to live in?

Life ABSOLUTES

Ok, you might be wondering if you can cut the pictures out of the book and use them as reminders …LOL…thanks for the idea. I have them for sale. All the pictures in this book are available for framing and hanging. Place them in your bathroom, kitchen, office study…when you do a private consult with me you get to take all the one-of-a-kind drawings home with you…even autographed ones. Most of my clients display them as reminders and inspiration ☺ Check them out on my website: www.masteringyourworld.com

TRUTHS RECAP: $[(e^E)\ T]A = \textbf{Outcome}$

- It is selfish to not fulfill my purpose in life.
- Mastery is the actual application of wisdom on a moment to moment basis…walking the walk.
- I choose to live a life of positive choices. Period!
- Everything happens for a reason, find the message and gain the knowledge and or wisdom! Thus, gain greater mastery.
- _____
- _____
  _____
  _____

Now then…You are on a roll!!! You are choosing to live a life full of positive experiences. Now, how about empowering yourself with the "know how" to not only set goals—also achieve them! Proceed to the next chapter ☺

CHAPTER 11

GOAL SETTING & ACHIEVING

DREAM SO BIG IT TAKES YOUR BREATH AWAY

We have goals that we have for our life, whether or not you're consciously aware of them. And some people are very good at setting goals and taking positive action, so they accomplish things very quickly. That's what makes successful people very successful, because they're constantly setting goals for themselves and acknowledging, as I mentioned before, the minute accomplishments. They are grateful! Celebrate life...all the moments in life...they all add up to the joy, abundance and success that empowers one to keep giving back to life! It's YOUR momentum.

"Efforts and courage are not enough without purpose and direction."
-John F. Kennedy
35th U.S. president, youngest person ever elected to the U.S. presidency

Goal setting happens first in your heart, where you can smell it, touch it, taste it, hear it, see it and feel it. Then in your mind where you can see it—visualize it, and then it must go onto paper for it to really have the power of your emotions, vision-thoughts to be fulfilled. This magnetizes your magnet for the entire universe to converge on your behalf in fulfilling your dream-goal. You are the one attracting and creating all the opportunities that allow your dream to come true. $[(e^E)\ T]A=O$.

TRUTH: There is no such thing as luck...luck is the opportunity you created. Creating/choosing the above choices allows the perfection that is you to "be," therefore manifesting almost instantly in your life! We call them miracles at times. When you have enough intense positive emotion, thought and action, the outcome appears to be a miracle. Once again, *"Ask and it shall be given," "Call unto me."* Asking-calling comes from the place of love. Charge your

Life ABSOLUTES

magnet with love! You will have uncountable miracles in your life.

Miracles are the way of life—not the exception. Remember the minute successes—are those not miracles too? That near miss of a car accident, missed bus, plane, train or appointment. That one right answer on the test that allowed you to pass...that last piece of chocolate you really wanted...I ask you...miracles? Everything in reality that is constructive is a miracle, therefore, miracles are the norm. Remember this—your life will be extremely blessed. Be grateful. Gratitude opens the door to abundance.

*"If you can **dream it**, you can **do it**."* -Walt Disney

So you're here, *X marks the spot in the drawing* and this is where you desire to be or obtain.

Sticking with the college theme, you desire to finish your college degree. Let's say you've been out of school for a long time and all of a sudden you realize your desire to go back to college and graduate.

So you're down on the bottom rung of the State of Success right now, and you want to start moving up. Well...

You tell a bunch of friends that you are going to go back to college to finish your degree and some of them are really supportive, but a lot of them say, *"Oh my goodness, you know how old you are and you are going back to college? You're really going to do that?"* blah, blah, blah... And right from the get-go you start feeling the fear and doubt. Your friends have triggered that self-talk of, *"Oh my goodness, I have fear and doubt now. I don't know. Can I really do*

Goal Setting & Achieving

this? I don't know. I really wasn't good in high school...the money, the time..."

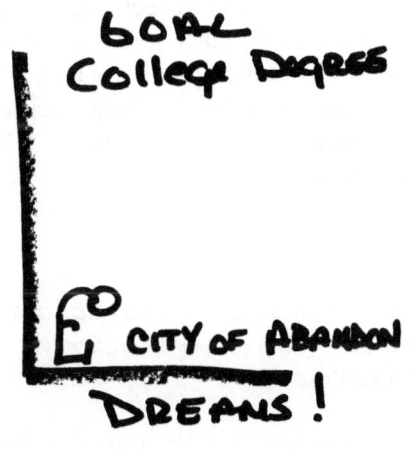

A lot of times you become paralyzed by the fear and you don't go any further, because you've already allowed the fear to step in and the doubt to step in.

So what is fear? It can be lack of information at times. Lack of love for self! Lack of love for others. Lack of courage to allow yourself to be great! This equals a trip to the City of Abandon Dreams.

In order to set dynamic goals, figure out what it is you want to achieve in life... know what it is you really want! I get this question a lot. How do I know what I want to do? Go back to your purpose in life.

What activities, passions do you have in your life that you just could not live without? Think of things that are constructive. You have all the money in the world, how are you living your days? What activities are you choosing to do?

Take those activities, those skills, that passion and find the career/activity that allows you to use them. The "job" does not exist? Then create it!

I have been self-employed the majority of my life. I started teaching when I was around 15 years old. People have always asked me to teach. I first taught baton, making twice what minimum wage is now, back then. I then taught in college when I was still a student, because a teacher of mine gave me encouragement and offered me the job. Again good money. Then I was asked (by my acting coach) to teach

Life ABSOLUTES

acting classes when I was training in Los Angeles, California. And here I am now, still teaching, still coaching.

Look at your life. There is a pattern...or one that has been attempting to form that is constructive. Yes, I have had other jobs. They all prepared me for the ones where I was self-employed. They all helped me gain knowledge. The reason I mention the money aspect of the careers I had is...**do what you love and the money will follow**! Enough about me for the moment.

Here is the truth about dreaming:

> *"Keep your dreams-intentions-goals in front of you every day and they are fulfilled through your pure joy and love of the journey."*
> -Karen LaVoie

TRUTH: Dream so big it takes your breath away!!! Literally, you dream so big that you stop breathing, your knees get weak, your eyes fill with water and you have this feeling that "terrifies" you! *You know that the voice inside of you called the wrong number.* Because the dream is bigger than you imagine you can achieve. It freaks you out! That can't be your plan in life!

TRUTH: In reality that is not terror or a wrong number! That is the feeling of greatness—the feeling of being alive! The knowing, finally, what it is that you are supposed to be and do every day—the activity that allows you to give joy, love, compassion and creativity to the rest of life. Every activity that is constructive is valuable to mankind. EVERY SINGLE ONE OF THEM!!! No matter your age! You are a part of the whole of this universe. You were born, therefore, you were invited to succeed in this lifetime—all the time. Period. NO EXCUSES.

> *"The biggest adventure you can ever take is to live the life of your dreams."* -Oprah Winfrey, O Magazine

All righty then, let's make an action plan—Goal Set.

Goal Setting & Achieving

You have already written down your Goal at the top of your goal list. Now ask yourself, what would you have done as an action step right before you completed your goal? The last step?

What happened when you attained that goal? You received your teaching degree! Write it down. What happened here? You took your finals? Write it down. Keep writing down the things you know. This is your fourth year of college. Somewhere in here is your third year of college. Somewhere in here is your second year of college. And down here, it's your first year of college.

Now, write these on your goal list—starting at the bottom…since you do rise up when you obtain and accomplish. So maybe the first step is that you check out the different colleges. After you check out the different colleges, then you decide what kind of program you desire to take. What your degree is going to be. Then you figure out what the cost is going to be. Then you figure out which college you desire to go to. Then you start college.

Then you say, *"I don't know. What happens after that? I don't know, because I've never been there…in here, where it is blank."* The EGO has named it the Fear and Doubt Zone. Dark and scary music plays in your head….worry creeps in…

And this is why most people fail at achieving what they desire in life. Because they say, *"I don't know what's going to happen here."* And so they don't start. If you don't start, then you can't fail. But did you?

TRUTH: You're failing still, because you're not going after what you desire. You're not going after what you desired—to go to college—because inside of you there's a passion that says, *"This is what I really desire to do."* That emotional core, that

Life ABSOLUTES

pure energy that flows into you tells you, *"This is what I really desire to do with my life!"* You can hear it as a voice inside your heart. *"This is what I really desire to do! This is part of how I fulfill my purpose in life."*

And so you talk about it, and you get excited but, oooh, scary music plays—so you don't do it. I've already failed before in life; I don't want to fail again. In reality, you're already failing for not starting, because you didn't follow through with what your passion in life is, what you really desired to do with your life. The only time a person fails is when they do not start and follow through. It is not failure when you truly change your mind. Perhaps the choice was only a stepping-stone that revealed to you that you really wanted to do something else. Then in reality you did complete the task at hand. Do you understand? Good!

Take action and see what Life/God reveals to YOU. Pursue every choice in life with passion, conviction and love for the opportunity to give. Then you will have a wonderful outcome that leads into another opportunity. That is what you do every day. You get up...perhaps before you ever get out of bed, you run through your head all the things you are going to do/accomplish in your day. Perhaps you even say, *"I am going to brush my teeth."* How many times have you been victorious at brushing your teeth? Every victory leads to another victory!!! Keep taking positive actions. Today is tomorrow and tomorrow will be today and there is ONLY NOW. Right NOW make tomorrow AWESOME!

So I'm here to tell you, if you go out and you check out the colleges, you check that off the list. Then you move onto the next step which is to figure out what program you desire to pursue—what degree you desire, and you check each of those off the list. While you're figuring out the program, you start gathering information about what's going to happen when you start college. YOU now know your classes. *"Ah! I get to put something more on my goal list! This is so exciting!"*

As you go forward in life you gain knowledge. And what is

Goal Setting & Achieving

knowledge? Knowledge is power—thank you—and it's also confidence! The human being just absolutely hungers for knowledge. It hungers for it. You are a sponge. That's why we have passion, because we desire more knowledge every single day. We're hungry for it. Figure out what you hunger for. When you start, you start gaining more knowledge, then more confidence. Once you gain more knowledge, you then gain more wisdom, and you just keep expanding your positive energy number as an individual. Knowledge becomes wisdom and wisdom becomes mastery. You gain MORE MASTERY as you go up in positive energy and you allow mastery to be.

Back to the goal...Part of the process of getting your teaching degree is that you figure out the cost, the location, the timing, etc. You figure out, *"Okay, now I know what college I desire to go to."* So then you have more information. Notice how we're just moving right through that so-called fear and doubt? It doesn't exist. Fear and doubt don't exist in reality. They never did, however you bought into it through your EGO. You put your attention on them. They don't exist in the positive world. You are now self disciplined, self-motivated, perhaps, self parenting and self paying your way through college and fulfilling your dream!

"Take the first step in Faith, you don't have to see the whole staircase, just take the first step." -Dr. Martin Luther King, Jr.

You keep going through the checklist. You just keep moving along. See how this works? You just keep moving along. You just keep moving along, because you might not know what's going to happen a month down the road until you get there. Right here, right now, you do what is required. Right here, right now creates what you get tomorrow. It creates what you get a week from now, and what you get a month from now, and a year from now.

Life ABSOLUTES

So right NOW, <u>you</u> choose to be passionate about making positive, constructive choices. You focus on what it is that you desire in your life. So whether it's your relationships, whether it's your job, whether it's your health, whether it's just about the overall happiness and joy in your life, you choose right here, right now, to focus on what it is that you desire, because it's a goal list.

It is a goal list! That's what you're doing every day; you're making a goal list of what you desire. What you desire in relationships. What you desire in your career. What you desire in your health. That's a goal list! You might not realize that's what you're doing, because few of us put it on paper and make the choices tangible. Be accountable. Do you think when you leave your goals in the ether that you supposedly never fail? Perhaps out of fear you are abandoning your dreams.

TRUTH: When making a goal list…keep it short for the day. You can sabotage yourself with goal lists. Write your goal list preferably around 7 pm the evening before. Only write down the Top 3 priorities. Get up the next day and complete those tasks before adding to your list. The EGO loves to sabotage. You make the list so long…you never start because you are so overwhelmed. Most of the items on the list are NOT that important. They are busy work to keep you from your dream…FEAR, DOUBT, WORRY…have crept into your list in the disguise of "to do" items. YES, YOU CAN LAUGH...even the best have allowed this to happen to them including me.

Make a habit of writing your goal list out before you turn in for the night. This habit will help prevent you from tossing and turning all night thinking about all the "stuff" that you have to do the next day. Also, knowing what you are going to accomplish the next day puts out positive energy about those things. While you are sleeping, you are attracting those solutions, people, opportunities, ideas. Your magnet is charged and attracting while you sleep. You are literally succeeding in your dreams while you are dreaming. Nice bonus!!!

Remember, your energy is always flowing.   **Action takes passion.**

Goal Setting & Achieving

Action takes powerful emotions. Setting goals fuels that passion! Do you realize you have thousands of thoughts every day and the only action you take is to not take action? Why? Fear or lack of passion are the two most likely culprits, or maybe because you are gaining mastery at being the authority over your world and you deleted them because they were destructive.

You are going "up the ladder" now that your goals are positive. Perhaps you flunk a test. You are required to study more—the appearance of a bump in the road...

Option #1 positive choice: You say, *"Maybe I'll go and get a tutor to help me. I'll talk to the instructor and ask for some extra schooling."* And you know what? When you go to that teacher you may feel like, *"I'm so embarrassed. I have to go and ask the teacher."* Go anyway...that is your ego talking—in reality what's going to happen to you? You never know. Maybe four years down the road when you graduate, that teacher's now your mentor and that teacher now helps you get the best job you can possibly have. That bump in the road was an opportunity for you to have an experience that was required in order to make this happen in your life down the road. That opportunity got you that letter of recommendation when you graduated from college, so that you were able to get that really great job. Everything has a reason. Everything "is" for a reason!

Option #2 negative choice: Seen as going sideways, "side tracking" on the goal setting drawing—taking the job that "sounds good" that was the quick fix for the EGO...City of Settle for Less...that can later turn into a downward spiral...City of Abandon Dreams.

Option #3 negative choice: Would be seen as heading downward on the goal setting drawing and ending up in the City of Abandon Dreams. You sit down and you stay angry about it and you have a pity party, and you drop out of school, you didn't get the lesson. You didn't get the lesson.

Quote from a client, who had already gone through my program, and who was attending a seminar.

Life ABSOLUTES

Client: *Can I share something? I had something happen to me about a month ago. Things were going really good. Work was good. We were moving into the _____, and I had a huge bump in the road, if you will. It involved personal and business, but it was a really big deal. And I took this (formula)—instead of the old way—I would have taken things, I would have cried, pouted, yelled, and probably accused everybody, gossiped, found everybody I could possibly find to take my side And that's human nature; that's what people do. — And especially with the circumstances, which I won't share.*

But this time I chose to say "You know, this has happened for a reason and I'm choosing to find the good in what is going to come out of this." And the people that were involved didn't take the same approach and they took the angry, the negative, the bad stuff out of everything and twisted it to where it was actually worse than what it really was. And I kept choosing to be positive and saying I'm going to learn something out of this, and stayed on my path for about two weeks, adamant not to go and self-destruct myself, because I easily, easily could have.

And I made some choices that I knew were going to affect people directly around me at work and in my family, and I stuck with that choice and believed in what I did, and my decision of what I did even made it so-called "worse" and I really stirred the pot and made things bubble, but I had to do what I believed in, knowing that something really, really good was going to come out of this ex-perience as "horrible" as it seemed living through it. And I didn't know what the outcome was going to be, and because I held my head high and I stayed strong and I believed I was going to learn something out of this, the result was so amazing and so incredible, and I —I'm going to get emotional I can tell—but if I would have stayed in that negative world and just went off to the wayside, I know I would have ended up just completely down in the gutter with it, and I would have lost completely with it. But instead, I won and I gained really good knowledge—and I'm sorry—well, I'm not sorry, but it's an emotional thing for me—but I actually ended up here and it came back ten times better. So what's she's saying is so true and so real. If people take the good, or the bad,   as what's coming and saying

Goal Setting & Achieving

there is something to be learned from this; honest to God it comes back way better if we don't let it go under that fear factor or that doubt.

Karen: Since you opened that door, can I just tell an overall perspective of what we did?

Client: *Yeah.*

Karen: What we did is, because this situation arose, I said, *"OK, what are the positive outcomes that you would like to happen? What are the positive outcomes you'd like to happen in your life because of this situation?"* And we made a list. We made a list: Plan A and Plan B. And these are the positive things that she desired to come out of that situation. And those choices could not hurt other people. Those choices weren't able to hurt other people because she was doing them from in here—her heart. She was doing them from a place of being a loving, giving, caring person. It works. Period.

Go ahead. Fire your EGO!!!

TRUTH: It's about you being happy so you can lift up everyone else around you. Until you get happy—you are cheating yourself and the rest of the world. Especially your loved ones!!! It is selfish to not achieve YOUR success in life.

First: What is your Dream? You can have as many as you want. Focus on your biggest one...it is usually family or career. Since we give the majority of our life energy to those activities it affects our health, relationships, finances and freedom of time.

What is your dream? Write it down!

Dream so BIG it takes your breath away!!! Stop reading right NOW and realize your dream! OK, right now...you can read again after you have written down your dream(s).

Now, write down why it is your dream. Why? The answer will be

Life ABSOLUTES

filled with a lot of emotionally charged words. Be as passionate as you can be. Yes, you might cry crocodile tears of joy while you are doing this and that is wonderful.

Grab your paper. NO EXCUSES. Write on the grocery bag…write. You have waited long enough. Success is a goal list away. Writing your list is a success on the way to many more successes in attaining your dream!!! Goal attaining is about momentum…remember the rocket…90% of it's fuel is used at blast off…this is you blasting off…**this is opportunity calling**…writing your goals…then you are in orbit on course and anything that comes along is an "hello" or an opportunity for more knowledge, wisdom and mastery. Write, write, write…STOP READING…PLEASE WRITE ☺ Don't think about it…FEEL about it!!! Write anything and everything.

The Miracle Mile by Erick Custodio -June 2006—One would think it to be "just" a two-week trip to L.A.. Connie and I felt so strongly that it would be a life changing two weeks as we held our breath when the plane touched down on the Bob Hope airport runway. The wheels squealed and we exhaled saying, "We're home."

Two years ago I walked in to Karen's Saturday workshop not knowing at the time that this energetic, positive, spiritual whirlwind of a woman would help me realize my dreams. Expecting to focus totally on acting it came as a surprise when Karen had us work on goal setting. What does this have to do with acting? Walking off that lane under the warm California sun we knew then that it had everything to do with acting. Everything we talked about, prayed about, prepared for and even dreamed about for two years happened in a matter of a week. To see those words written down when we thought it was just an exercise at the time come to life right before our eyes was absolutely amazing.

Karen's keen understanding of the TRUTH that talent alone can take you so far and that business savvy is a necessary tool for success in the industry helped us get to where we are now. Not only were we ready to perform in the L.A. market but we were ready to do

Goal Setting & Achieving

business in the L.A. market... cont.

TRUTHS RECAP: $[(e^E)\ T]A = $ **Outcome**

- Until I get happy—I am cheating myself and the rest of the world. Especially my loved ones!!! It is selfish to not achieve MY success in life.
- I will dream so big that it takes my breath away!
- I will goal set and achieve by taking one step at a time knowing the next action will be revealed to me.
- *Keep your intentions-goals in front of you every day and they are fulfilled through your pure joy and love of the journey –Karen LaVoie*
- I will update my goal list the night before with only three items to accomplish and then the next day I will accomplish them.
- _____
  _____
  _____
  _____
- _____
  _____
  _____
  _____
  _____
- _____
  _____
  _____
  _____

CONGRATULATIONS!!! Now you are on your way. You are going to want more paper to write down all the miracles that keep happening in your life and everything you are grateful for. This list will be long and well worth it!

Life ABSOLUTES

"Karen has given me a new perspective on how to approach the creative aspects of my work. She's enlightened our production company creatively and given us important tools that we can utilize on a regular basis that will assist us in achieving our goals and success." -Patrick Lamb-musician/song writer/singer
http://www.patricklamb.com

"Karen LaVoie's book, Life ABSOLUTES, really helped me learn how to use and apply complicated spiritual principles to my everyday life. For example, I read Karen's book while I was interviewing for a full time position at the William Morris Agency and used some of her <u>visualization</u> and Law of Attraction ideas throughout my interview process to help me get the job. Thank you for sharing your wisdom and experiences."

In Gratitude,
Matt Welsh, Author of The Bottom Line
www.followyourpassiontoday.com

To add the finishing touches to your goal accomplishing skills I want you to learn and apply the power of Visualization to this process. So go to the next chapter and hold on to your seat…you are going to be amazed at how masterful you really are!

CHAPTER 12

THE POWER OF VISUALIZATION

THE FINAL TOUCH

"...I am flying a kite on a warm Spring day—the smell of flowers wafts under, around and into my nose, my heart, my ears...the smell of freshly cut grass and the giggle of the little girl inside me effortlessly coming forth and floating off into eternity. The kite sails with the joy of freedom and the happy expressions of being alive...oh, the freedom of life! A butterfly floats by enjoying the grandeur of God's abundance and glory...the suns rays are bright and yet not blinding, warm and embracing like the touch of a loving embrace...all is in perfection in God's kingdom—Heaven on Earth."

Did you see that image? Did you experience it? Could you smell, feel, hear, see and taste it? It is simply written in a matter of less than a minute. The Power of Visualization has been touted for years. Why? —because it works!

I consciously started using visualization in the 1970's. Was visualization taught back then? Well, I was not told about it. It came to me powerfully one day. Visualize what it is you want to accomplish. See yourself already having accomplished it perfectly! Made sense to me. What was I doing? I was a competitive baton twirler. A lot of the tricks I did in my routine were unique—I was the only one doing them. So in order to see them done correctly I visualized myself doing them. I saw myself doing my whole routine perfectly—all my routines perfectly. It did not matter how my competition looked. It was how I looked and felt. Mostly how I FELT! I wanted to feel confident. Let's face it. The opposite of Confident is FEARFUL. That would not get me my perfect routine or most importantly the feeling of joy—FUN!

I loved to perform when I was confident, otherwise it was not fun....down right nerve racking! Long story short...it paid off!!!

Life ABSOLUTES

So what does this have to do with you? Simple, you want to feel good all the time. YOU want to be more successful.

TRUTH: The most powerful way to attract perfection to you is to put the final touches on your dreams. SEE and FEEL yourself already there!!! Remember, the NOW creates your tomorrow. Contemplate this every day it will open up so many doors. Feel and see perfection in your minds eye, get excited about it, be grateful for it!

OH, now you understand this statement more. Now, you understand why you have heard people say, *"You have to be there before you can get there."* The EGO really got you frustrated over that comment...perhaps you said, *"Duh!!! If I was already there then I wouldn't be here."* EXACTLY!!!

YOU are where you direct your emotionally charged thoughts, and actions. YOUR ATTENTION. Got it? Please remember, action does include speaking the spoken word. To empower your dream, your vision—speak the truth of it. *I am this, I am that*...make sure they are constructive statements.

Now, the simple and POWERFUL formula to visualizing is this—write it down—write down all the wonderful feelings, smells, taste, sounds and experiences you will enjoy while accomplishing your big dream and once you're there! The more passionate you are the more power you have. Put yourself in that reality NOW. Remember, emotion is the power that keeps you motivated, thus, propelling you forward and at the same time drawing the end result to you faster. YOU are a magnet for what you put out! Once again, this is the Law of Attraction—Manifesting.

This is how I teach actors how to become a role—how to embody that performance flawlessly, singers, athletes...all my clients.

"All the world is a stage." -William Shakespeare

Life is your stage. Be that which you truly want to be!

The Power of Visualization

TRUTH: Actors are those seeking the truth of their being.

So write down your dream. Remember dream BIG! Some people say they cannot visualize. That is not true. We do it all day long. Whenever you say you are going to do something, you see it in your mind's eye. We use the expression *"I see"* when someone is telling us something. The TRUTH is, when you dream too small the truth of your being will not show you that vision because it wants you to know you dreamed too small. When you dream big, it really does take your breath away. You realize that that which is greater than anything of man, that which is going to be the power, the doer, the giver, the creator within you that makes that dream come true. **Always acknowledge that "Life" gave you everything constructive in your world primarily—not mankind. Yes, life quite often uses humans as vessels to give that which you require for your success.** However, it was not the human creating the gift it was life. God's life. God's love.

Keep writing your dream(s) down until they are so vivid…take longer than a minute, take hours or days until there is nothing missing. Fill in every detail as much as you can. You say you don't know—then do as much as you can. YOU get to come back to this dream, vision and add to it as information is revealed to you on your journey. This process is transformational. You are a higher being every day when you live the truth within in this book every day! The awesome thing is—things that you did not dream of will be added. That's the bonus of being willing to dream and pursue your dream. You attract greatness, abundance, creativeness, knowledge, opportunities. Doors open that you —your EGO—never thought possible, just because you dared to dream. YOU dared to be more than so-called possible. I am here to tell you, when you can dream it then somewhere in the Universe it is possible.

Is it practical? Is it constructive? Does it better mankind? Choose wisely. You are accountable for your choices. People can play the EGO game and think of absurd things and waste their life energy to sabotage their real dreams. Why do they do that? FEAR.

Life ABSOLUTES

All the greatest achievers in the world dared to dream bigger than others. Your dream is as big as you want it to be for you—NO one else. It is your dream. You can hear it in your heart. It makes your hands sweat, your body tremble, your heart race and you feel alive…write it down.

"Karen LaVoie is an Overwhelming and Awesome individual. In my own life experience it is not often when I have encountered and become friends with anyone who exudes and emanates more Positive Polarity, Uplifting energy than Karen LaVoie.

In "Life ABSOLUTES" Karen presents a simple and guided step by step program by which anyone can transform their life and affairs. Get Your Own Copy of this book. Proceed through all of the steps which Karen clearly outlines in each of the chapters.

Then watch your life transform itself into that Joyous and Happy Bliss we were all intended to experience from the day we began our journey from birth in this lifetime. May you all be Blessed with Abundant Health, Infinite Prosperity, Eternal Divine Love and all the Joyous Activities of your own Divine Plan Fulfilled. Thank you to my dear friend Karen."

Sincerely Devoted "I AM" Student of Beloved Saint Germain *(name withheld by request)*

Write YOUR dreams down NOW.

The Power of Visualization

Keep writing!

"I have really been getting into character when I sing at gigs. It is crazy what just a bit of focus and imagery can do...your suggestions were very helpful and inspiring."
-Ms. B -Belinda Underwood – singer/musician

CONGRATUALTIONS! Now, read it, feel it, smell it, touch it, taste it, hear it and <u>visualize</u>/experience it every chance you get. Keep it to yourself. Keep it safe from the dream stealers of the world. Your emotionally charged dream is the place that your energy attracts to. It is your magnet. It is your calm, peaceful lake that is like a mirror that allows you to see vividly your future, which is right NOW.

Life ABSOLUTES

"Imagination is everything. It is the preview of life's coming attractions." -Albert Einstein

Remember you must BE there before you get there. Read your "vision" statement when you wake up in the morning and visualize it. Experience it! Embrace it! Feel the power it sends through your being, listen to the insight and inspiration it tells you. Own it. Expect it and accept it. Allow the NOW of its being to give you more and more confidence to journey every day in the actions required to attain this goal-dream. Read it before going to sleep and use the same process. When you go off to sleep, the life energy that flows through you will keep acting on your behalf without any of your conscious restrictions, and it will go out and bring to you that which you require to accomplish your dream.

Note: I did not say visualize then do nothing! I said take action based on the inspiration of the experiencing of your vision. Positively driven thoughts and actions = Positive outcome. ☺ Driven by Positive EMOTIONS!

This is also very useful. Should there be a day when you have the so-called bump in the road, air turbulence, opportunity knocking and you want to give into negative emotions…read your vision statement. It is your flagger too.

Should you be so inspired, you can make a vision wall in your home, office or a vision board that has pictures, sayings and goals. Whatever inspires you to keep being passionate, focused, inspired and taking action. Does this sound like what huge corporations do in order to stay successful? BE Alert…wonderful blessings will drop in from seemingly nowhere. Miracles. Opportunities. Be Alert!

TRUTH: This is not lying to yourself; it is about building your confidence in what you are in reality already able to do. You just haven't yet taken the actions required to confirm that truth. It has been said, *"It is the universe conspiring on your behalf or converging"*…well, yes!!! YOU are the magnet!!! You get back what you put out. The universe is limitless in energy. By you using

The Power of Visualization

it constructively you are expanding it....how cool is that!!!

You can sit there and make up silly stories and hypotheticals all day long as to why this is wrong. You are right, your dreams won't happen because there is fear and doubt attached to them, your hypotheticals do not have enough desire, intense emotion or action in order to make them happen. Those who argue this proven truth are those in the City of Abandon Dreams. Your EGO has become your ruler and until you take charge you will live in lack and limitation and be dictated to by your fears and doubts. The truth hurts. I call it like it is. It was the medicine that woke me up. Truth can hurt because the EGO lets it, and when it hurts enough you decide to get out. There is only ONE real way to get out and that is to love others and love yourself enough to start dreaming again and make your dreams happen and be grateful!

Now, for the FEARLESS and courageous—keep Visualizing!!! It works for everything you want. Remember, this is about positive visions and your world...you cannot force others to be in your world. Your vision must be unselfish!

Use it, Use it, Use it and use it more! Think about this formula the next time you watch a movie. The movie had to be visualized before it could be made. The pencil had to be visualized before it was created. Everything has been created twice—once in the invisible (visualized) and again in the visible.

You might be saying I did not visualize this bad thing happening in my life. Did you ever have fear about it? Did you ever discuss it, did you ever see it happen on T.V. or a movie...hear about it? Then you had the vision. This is why it is so important to stand guard of what you are taking into your world through your senses. I could write a separate book on this topic alone and perhaps I will.

TRUTH: YOU are the creator of your world. You are gaining greater mastery by applying this simple law of love. Love your dreams. Love the journey. Love the minute accomplishments of every day and be grateful for all that comes from the experiences of

Life ABSOLUTES

your life. You are the master of your life energy. To MORE success!!!

Want a bit of inspiration? Watch one of the following movies: *"Finding Neverland," "Rudy," "Dreamer," "A Beautiful Mind," "The Rookie," "The Wizard of Oz," or "The Matrix"* just to name a few...really watch them with your heart! Checkout: www.spiritualcinema.com.

Also, "The Star Wars" series is so dialed into the knowing, *"one must master their emotions in order to be a master Jedi,"* is mentioned several times! (I paraphrased the dialogue from Star Wars)

Why did he turn to the dark side? He did not follow the formula!

TRUTHS RECAP: $[(e^E) \, T]A = $ **Outcome**

- I am reading and visualizing my dream statement/vision statement every night before I go to sleep and every morning when I awake!
- I am aware of what I am watching on TV or in movies and aware of what I am listening to!
- This is MY dream!!! I own it in my life right here right NOW.
- _____

Let's keep your momentum going!!! Sometimes you might be sabotaging yourself—read on to find out.

CHAPTER 13

THE SILENT KILLERS

LANGUAGE AND BEHAVIOR THAT DESTROYS

YOU are so excited and dialed in—let me help you avoid sabotaging yourself with the silent killers. *"Sticks and stones may break my bones but words can never hurt me."* Well, I grew up believing that for many years. Not so. **Words do hurt. Words can kill.** Words go out and can NEVER be called back!

Let me tell you a story about a woman named Karen, yes me, not the present me. (I talk in third person about negative topics to avoid attracting them into my life.)...At one stage in Karen's life, she decided she should be a social person even though she was really shy. At the time, the social thing to do was to go out and get together with people and sit around and have conversation. Well, what those conversations ended up being, mostly, was gossip and complaining. (hmm, isn't this still the same thing that people do?) The conversations ended up being about what people were jealous about or unhappy about—and Karen was happy in her relationship, career, finances and her health, so she really didn't have anything to contribute. Life was really good. Everything was going her way. But her "friends" had stuff to complain about.

Well, once again, she wasn't involved in their "group." She was on the outside. So in order to be a part of that "group," to fit in, she decided to create things to complain about. When you look hard enough, you can create something. So she decided to start finding things to complain about so she could be a part of her friends' little social gatherings. And so then, it became the gossip, complain game.

Life ABSOLUTES

So what happened was very silently and very deadly. (Now you're world is a boat.) Every time that Karen gossiped or complained, it was like a little barnacle attaching to her boat. And over a period of time, the boat—Karen's world—started collecting barnacles.

It was still afloat, of course. Things were still going pretty well. They weren't going quite as well as they had been a couple years before, and everybody said, *"That's the way it goes."* You have your highs and lows in life, and Karen bought into that. Eventually, her boat had so many barnacles attached to it that a huge hole was created in it and it sank. A car accident was the sinking of her boat. The "sudden storm" that capsized it! Image 44

The car accident, according to the police report, was not Karen's fault. She got rear ended. But in reality, she couldn't have been in that place had she not put out that energy to put herself in that place to attract that accident that happened to her. Karen was accountable for putting herself in that place by creating that energy that put her

The Silent Killers

there. Now that might be "kind of far out there" for you, that's the truth of it. She got into a bad accident. At that moment had she known what I know now—she could have just said, *"What's the lesson here? What shall I do to change in my life?"* The message could have been as simple as, *"I was tired and I knew not to get on the road today. My inner voice was telling me not to drive."* Sometimes, the lesson is, LISTEN TO YOUR INNER VOICE! It warned you didn't it? Note, I said inner voice ☺ Once again this is not a scapegoat or an easy way out. What is your inner knowing telling you, not your EGO?

Before that accident, Karen had been in four other car accidents, none of them her fault. Her car had now been rear ended five times. Constantly, "life" was attempting to give her wake-up calls....her "hello's." None of the car accidents were her fault according to human laws.

So the last barnacle that absolutely sank Karen's boat was accident number five. At that point she was underwater, and was literally drowning. One night she didn't want to be on the planet. She did not know how to come up for air. She couldn't breathe. And Karen got to that place because of gossip, complaining, judging, fault finding, selfishness, FEAR and doubt. Even though she was an extremely fearless person when it came to taking risks, Karen's fears were in other areas. They started attracting negative things into her life. They started tearing her apart and it built to the point that Karen was jealous of other people—Karen opened herself up to negative emotions, by telling herself, *"Let's tear them apart. What's wrong with their business so Karen can make her business look better?"* *"What's better about me over that person so Karen can say she is better?"* *"That person drinks too much."* Karen was finding fault in others in order to make herself look better, when in reality it was destroying her. Putting down others or finding fault, so that she could have a quick fix, was destroying her life.

It was destroying Karen, because she was becoming more and more angry. Karen was becoming more defensive. She was feeling as though she had less worth. The more Karen was tearing down other

Life ABSOLUTES

people, the more she was tearing down herself. Karen felt worthless. She started having a lot of doubt in herself. She started worrying about her money. Her whole world started to deteriorate—her relationships went bad. Her world just self-destructed around her and the rest of the world didn't know it. Karen could put a smile on her face and be in absolute horrible, horrible emotional pain inside. Karen self destructed. Now did Karen make bad choices all day long? NO, they add up! The silent killers add up!

And out of the ashes of self destruction rose the Phoenix that is Karen today.

Number one past-time, in my opinion, in the world, is gossip—and when I say gossip, that doesn't mean kind conversation about another person. I am talking about conversation where we are picking other people apart, where we're finding fault in somebody. This is what we do when we have social hours. This is what we do, the majority of the time, when we go out after work and have a couple of cocktails. This is what we do when we go home and talk to our friends on the phone, or we stand around the water cooler, wherever it is, talking about the faults of other people usually behind someone's back.

Image 45

The Silent Killers

Gossiping and complaining, judging and criticizing are acceptable in our society. It's acceptable behavior and that's what we do. We get together and we complain about the things going on in our world or we gossip about what's wrong with somebody else—what's happening in their world that's so horrendous and so terrible. We gossip about our government officials, our parents, our spouse, our family members, church members, co-workers, our neighbors. You know what? Don't go there. You don't want your ship to sink. I offer it to you; don't go there. It's similar to playing in quicksand. You have plenty to take care of with yourself and plenty of positive places to put your attention.

When there's something in a person that you, in your perception think should be changed, you see that, then take the action to help them. Or better yet, send them positive emotionally driven thoughts! This will help anyone tremendously!!! Send them LOVE! Help make their life easier instead of harder by sending negative energy. Because I'm here to tell you, you have an accountability for all that negative energy that you put out, judging those other people, because that energy went out and affected their world. You put that negative energy onto them. Now whether they accepted it or not, was their choice. You are accountable, not only for your life, but for that person's life, you helped destroy. You are accountable for that. Lots of "hellos" were had when Karen started her new positive life.

One of the elements of gossip is judgment. We are judging. That person's too tall. That person's too short. That person's too bald. That person's too fat. That person's too old. That person's too young. That person's too stupid. That person's too smart. That person's too—blah, blah, blah. You know what? Allow people to be who they want to be because we have freedom to be who we want to be. Now that does not mean people get to break the law. They break the law, they break the law. Be a part of the solution. Do not sit and condemn. Their "human" obviously, as I stated before, requires more love. And when you choose to find fault in them, you're only creating negative in your world. All in all, all the negatives tie together and slowly you will destroy your world by taking on more and more negative habits, just like Karen did. All of those bad habits

Life ABSOLUTES

go slowly, undetected until your boat sinks! Silent and Deadly!

So now my mission in life is to be the person who goes out and uplifts other people like you. The person who goes out and gives you positive, constructive ways to change your life; to fulfill the passion and desire that you have in life; to help you be the person who loves who you are; to really love who you are; to really be excited about what it is that you do in your life.

When you gossip about other people, you're putting out negative things about that person. You're not helping them by gossiping about them. You want to help somebody, say, *"You know what? From where I stand, this is going on in your life. I would like to help you because you have a choice. This is what I would like to do. Would you like that assistance?"* Remember they get to choose. Be careful. Are they really doing something destructive or is it <u>all</u> <u>about</u> <u>your</u> EGO?

When we love other people, they say *"Cool, other people love me and it feels good."* You're gossiping about somebody, they would say, *"Ugh, other people are gossiping about me."* So they start spiraling down.

When somebody asks you something, and you don't have anything positive to say, I have this wonderful comeback: I say, *"What do you think?"* At some point in time you will figure out how to walk away from those conversations. You want to learn how to walk away from those people who like to gossip, who like to judge, who like to make those negative choices. Start walking away from them. Start walking away from them! And it might seem like you're losing your friends: they're not friends when they want you to stay in negative energy. They're not your friends. As you get more confident you will state, *"I choose not to gossip, judge...let's change the subject."* ☺

Stay away from judging and gossip. When your boat sinks you'll be aware of how big a supply of negative energy there is in your world. All of a sudden your job goes bad. Your relationships go bad. Your health goes bad—you don't have health insurance on top of it, now

The Silent Killers

that you lost your job! It'll sneak up and "slap you upside of the head" one day!

I've lived through these experiences and know the effects of them. They're silent and deadly. Silent and deadly! Because you don't necessarily see the negative effect from them right away, so you think it's OK, until one day, your life is absolutely in a place of disaster —completely turned upside down!

That wonderful saying that we were told way back when, *"when you don't have anything nice to say, don't say anything at all,"* is true!

That doesn't mean that your employer or that "somebody" isn't able to tell you something about yourself that they would like to have you improve upon. When somebody says, *"I would like you to do this better,"* that's that validity factor. Does it have validity? *"Yes! I should be doing that better. Yes, thank you."* That's constructive because they're helping you get to a better place. It's not judgment for the sake of being mean and malicious and tearing somebody apart.

Are you talking badly about your partner? You are accountable for the actions that you take in relationships. Your relationship isn't working, ask yourself why? Be accountable for your actions. You're not doing well at your job, why? Be accountable for your actions at your job. It's not about what Sally or Joe or what everybody else is doing. Your finances are in the toilet, ask why? Be accountable for what you're doing with your finances. The same thing with your health—be accountable.

That's what life is about: being accountable for whatever it is in your life, and being accountable in a positive way, because, you know what? You don't want your hand held; you don't like being micro-managed in life. So when you're accountable, those things go away because people realize that you are accountable. You feel like you're being micro-managed in your life, in your relationship, in your job, in whatever it is, you feel like you're being micro-managed, ask yourself, why? Maybe you're not being accountable. Perhaps you are

Life ABSOLUTES

giving your power away to others. Are you playing the victim?

When you feel unworthy people will take advantage of you! So people feel a desire to tell you everything you should do in your life. Did you pick up your socks? Did you put the toilet seat down? Did you—you know those things. Obviously, the accountability hasn't been there, so they keep at you—what we call nagging or parenting or bossing. Make sure there is a constructive balance from ALL parties involved.

Let me point out in a list the silent yet deadly killers of life:
- Gossip
- Judgment
- Jealousy
- Hate
- Bragging
- Criticism

…which lead to:
- Defensiveness
- Lying
- Cheating
- Loneliness
- Doubt
- Addictions

AND MANY MORE…a very negative human portrait: Not to mention the language we use!!! Yes, they all tie together and have facets that are similar to each other. FEAR and doubt created them, hate propels them and selfishness sustains them. These are immortalized in our movies, T.V. shows, books, newspapers, schools, jobs and every-day conversations.

Gossip is destructive because it's not The Truth. And even when it is the truth, gossip, in the form of gossip I'm referencing is negative. You're talking about finding fault in somebody else. Finding fault in somebody else for the sake of finding fault—tearing down another human being! What's good about gossip in the minds

The Silent Killers

of people, it makes them feel better about themselves—for a moment.

For a moment, say you find fault in that person, thing or situation, then you feel better about yourself. I'm here to tell you it's a quick fix. It is a quick fix! Because after you've found fault in that person, what happens is you know that somebody else is finding fault in you—because you set the stage. You sent it out to the universe, and you're going to get it back. Say you're going around finding fault in everybody else, well, then you get paranoid: everybody else is judging me. Then you get on the defensive and you just spiral down. And the thing with gossip is you destroy other people's lives, it's the telephone game. When it starts and when it gets back to wherever it's supposed to be going to, it's been so distorted with so much negative information, that you could have absolutely ruined somebody's life. You are accountable for that. You're accountable! You cannot call words back. When you put out bad information, you put out rumors, you spread gossip; you're accountable for destroying somebody else's life. That was your choice. You made that choice to let those things come out of your mouth. Those things then went out and destroyed somebody's life, and you're accountable for that. Hopefully, this statement alone will get you to think twice about your thoughts and spoken words/actions.

Yes, your thoughts that are negative go out to that which your attention is on when they are powerful and focused...which does not take much energy at all. This includes worrying! Guess what? Whether you speak the thoughts out loud or not they have power! Spoken or unspoken, you are creating in YOUR world and affecting all of life. That is why I stress, be aware of your EMOTIONS. Nip the negative ones in the bud!

Perhaps you see what you believe should be changed in a person. The only time you may point that out is when you think that you can do something to help them. You're going to do something constructive to help them, then that becomes a positive thing. Otherwise, wish them well in your heart and move on. Sometimes that is the best thing to do in a situation. You will know by using the

Life ABSOLUTES

formula what the constructive option is.

People, who are miserable in their lives, are going to find fault in everybody and his brother, because they get a quick fix. *"I'm better than them. I'm better than them."* They're pulling their energy down further and further and further...Pity Party!

You see somebody on the street and you say, *"That person's homeless. What can I do to help?"* That's a positive thing. When you say, *"I can't believe that person's on the street just mooching off of life—nyah nyah nyah,"* you're making a negative choice.

TRUTH: The damage of gossip, judgment, fault finding—it's really hard to fix, because the seed has been planted and the damage has been done. Sometimes it's fixable, sometimes it isn't. Easy solution, BE the solution! See only the good in people, places and things. Not enough positive there? Then move on! Move out! Take a positive action! Get out! Choose to live in the positive!

Let's talk about bragging. Bragging is taking credit for the "human" having accomplished something. Once again, the human is that which is the EGO. Well, by now you realize the human does nothing that is constructive—the human element is the EGO. That which gives you life is what allows you to do something wonderful in the first place. So instead of bragging, give praise and gratitude to life. Then you keep the flow of positive energy coming your way. The moment you claim anything good as your own you just shut the door on your abundance coming in because you put your focus on the EGO.

Our language—our society uses words including *hate*, *sorry*, *need*, *try*, *have to*, *can't*, and *if* because the ego wants to be right all the time. The ego wants to be right all the time! You already know about potty mouth words that are now acceptable in our society (words that were not acceptable 10 years ago), and using God's name in vain. Does that tell you our society as a whole is spiraling down? We have lowered our standards to feel better about ourselves. Our society has justified our lower standards by saying,

The Silent Killers

"It's called freedom of speech. It's called slang. It's called, I'm not all uptight and proper and stuffy. I'm not a goody two-shoes."

TRUTH: The EGO is lying to YOU. Potty mouth is Degradation—also known as immorality.

We're taught about four-letter words when we're children. Not to use them, yes? The word hate should have been at the top of the list. **Hate** is an extremely volatile, destructive, emotionally charged word. So when something happens in your world, your attention is on it, and you decide to have hate about it, you're destroying your life with huge amounts of negative energy. And, not only are you destroying your life, you're helping to destroy the lives of people around you, because you're taking that negative energy and dumping it on them, making it more difficult for them to stay in their positive place.

Some have the habit of saying, *"I hate potatoes."* You don't hate potatoes. You'd rather have an orange. You don't hate the potato. When you say the word "hate" you're putting a massive amount of negative energy out into your world making your life a whole lot more difficult. You're attracting all the things that you "hate" in your life back into you—in greater amounts. Greater amounts! And you're creating greater amounts of hate in the world. You are attracting back everything that has the same vibration of hate in the world. Think about it! Do you really want all that in your world? War is created by hate energy.

You say, *"I hate being fat."* Guess what happens? You get fatter. You get fatter because your attention is on being fat, and what you focus on you get more of. *"I hate being poor,"* you're focusing on being poor; you get poorer because you're putting your attention on it, with intensely charged "hate" energy, thus, attracting it back to you at a high rate of speed!

We say, *"Oh, I hate when I hit a red light! I hate it when the cookie crumbles. I hate it when this happens! I hate it when I stub my toe!"* No, you don't hate it. You wish that it wouldn't have happened, but it's not hate. Hate is the opposite of love. The complete opposite of

Life ABSOLUTES

love.

When you're saying you hate something, you're putting the biggest glop of negative energy behind whatever it is that you say you hate. *"I hate my job!"* Well, you're just asking for trouble. You're asking for trouble, because that energy just went out there, and your day is going to be a really BIG "Hello!" day.

OK? So take the word hate out of your vocabulary. Hate is selfishness and selfishness/hate creates wars! That energy accumulates to a certain point then a war is created. Why do the same areas of the world have war? Because the energy is still in the atmosphere over the earth in that area just waiting for an opening to come forth and be active through human channels.

Then there is the word **sorry**. Sorry is a very negative word; it comes from sorrow. Let us say somebody has passed away and their relative or friend is doing better about moving on and dealing with their feelings. Somebody comes up and says, *"I am so sorry."* What happens is that person might start bawling again because you took their attention and put it back on where they didn't want their attention to be—on the "sorrow," Just because you said, *"I'm sorry."* They were doing so well until that you said, *"I'm sorry,"* and then they lost it because you put that negative energy on them, you drew their attention over onto the "sorrow" exactly where they didn't want it to be.

So in that kind of situation say, *"I'm here to support you. I'm here to be a friend."* That's a positive thing. It's uplifting. It gets the person moving through that situation.

Sympathy is also negative because when you sympathize with somebody, you're actually going into that negative place with them. You're having a pity party with them. I know that sounds odd, because that's the vocabulary we've been told to use. We go out and get cards that say "in deepest sympathy" and "deepest sorrow" and all you're doing is adding to that person's challenge of moving up and out of that experience in their life.   You're making it harder for

The Silent Killers

them. So, instead say, *"I'm here for you as a friend. I'm here to help you have happiness in your life again."* Focus on the positive things with them.

When you say in sorrow, *"Oh, I'm so sorry!"* and you hug them, all you did was just envelope them in a whole bunch of extra negative energy. What you did is subconsciously say, *"I want you to feel more pain. Go ahead and stay in that pain."*

By giving compassion, you're allowing them to rise out of that and heal themselves. Compassion is love, and love heals the human emotional core. Love heals everything that's destructive in our emotional core, because it just feels so doggone good. It feels so good and it heals all. Love is a very high rate of vibration…greater absorbs the lesser.

You want to give that person love, and you want to uplift them. You want to help the pain go away and by saying that you're sorry, you're only adding to the pain. You're doing the opposite thing of what you think you're doing. And that's why some people, in an odd way, are very wise—they move away from everybody when something really traumatic happens in their life. In reality, sometimes that's the best thing when everybody's bombarding them with *"I'm so sorry; I'm so sorry!"*

Note: Laughter in your own traumatic situation is the healthiest response a person can experience. The laughter raises one out of the negative hold of the situation!!! Laughter is a natural healer of emotional pain! Laugh right now…go ahead laugh…start laughing…feels good doesn't it? Laughter is a quick pick me up you can give yourself anytime you want. Just LAUGH at yourself!!! ☺

Feel free to say to people *"Please, do me the huge favor—stop saying that word 'sorry,' because all that does is make me work harder to get out of that place. It gives me more to work through. You're dumping more negative energy onto my situation. Thank you for understanding."*

Life ABSOLUTES

Different sorry situation. When somebody comes up and says, *"I am so sorry that I did that to you!"* Does that make you feel better? No. *"What's that all about? I'm not going to feel sorry for you."* However, when someone says, *"Will you please forgive me? I want to apologize,"* that makes you feel better! Because they are saying that they made a mistake.

They are saying at that moment it was the right choice; at this moment, I now know it was not the best choice that I made and I'd like to correct that. So, replace *"sorry"* with *"I apologize. Forgive me. I made a mistake."* That is more pleasing-positive. Oh, they just admitted they made a mistake. *"OK,"* you say to yourself, *"I am good with that. Thank you."* You get it? Positive energy negates the negative or better yet, avoids it all together.

TRUTH: People use the words "I'm sorry" carelessly. *"I'm sorry!"* No you're not. Be aware of how many times you use that word. It is a word that people with low self esteem use a lot —a habit worth changing.

The other words people say are, *"I am so stupid. I am so ugly. I am so fat. I am such a loser."* You're declaring that into your world. You're putting 100% of your focus on exactly what you do not want. When you're saying *"I am this"* and it's something negative, you're taking all your energy and putting it on that quality or situation.

You're declaring that to yourself, to life and to everybody around you that that's what you are or who you are. When somebody comes up to you, how do you expect them to feel about you when you keep saying, *"I'm so stupid, I'm so stupid?"* That's the perception they're going to get because that's what you put out. That's what **you** put out. That's what you declared in your world.

Now, say, *"I am smart. I am better. I am happier. I am healthier. I am more successful. I am making more money."* Talk about the positive things that you're choosing to have in your life, not the negative things that you're eliminating. Let go. That's right: Just throw them away. I have my clients visualize this big dump truck.

The Silent Killers

We just back it up to my office. We just shovel it all in there and we send it off to the dump, never to be seen again. What's in the past is in the past. Looking in the past and going, *"OH, I can't believe I did all those things,"* is just putting your focus on things that have already happened. I'm here to tell you, all there is, is right here, right now. Right here, right now. Whatever you choose RIGHT NOW is what creates in the next right here, right now. In the next right here, right now, so choose wisely! You can choose to be the person who turns on the high beams and only looks ahead, or you can choose to be the person who is constantly looking in the rearview mirror. Who do you think is going to move forward in life? You can't move forward when you're constantly looking back.

Be careful when you're saying, *"I am,"* because it declares into your existence. Be aware of what you're saying. Make sure it's something positive and constructive. *"I'm happy. I'm joyous. I'm in love. I'm getting my perfect health. I'm healthier. I'm happier. I'm attracting more money."* Remember? What do you want in your life? Focus on talking about the things that are getting better, not about what you don't want. **Focus on what you do want and have**. When you share with the world what you want, doors open, because somebody says, *"I know somebody who can help you with that!"*

When you talk about what you like in life, people can help you achieve that. We like helping other people achieve things they like. I like to call it—you're a "glue person." You're the person who knows somebody that can help somebody. You hook them together. You're the "glue person," helping people have opportunities in their lives. Remember, your life is perfect. Accept that you're perfect, that is the spiritual allowing and letting go! I am happy. I am wealthy. I am healthy. I am _____. Focus on the truth of perfection.

> ***"Do** or do not, there is no try."*
> Yoda-Jedi master, from the "Star Wars" series

Try. Yet another word we have been told to remove from our vocabulary. The challenge for most people is what word to use

Life ABSOLUTES

instead of "try." Let me give you some suggestions. *"I did my best"*—instead of *"I tried." "I called you and you were not there,"* in place of *"I tried to get a hold of you." "I will give it my all"* instead of *"I'll try."* Figure out your "truth words" to say and use.

Have to…this might be the first time you have heard this one. Stop saying *I have to*. You do not "have to" do anything: not pay your taxes or even die. That is another whole book. You have the freedom to choose, you do not "have to." You do however have to deal with the consequences of your choices! That is a definite "have to!" That is the Law of cause and effect.

TRUTH: I get to go to my job. I get to mow the lawn. I get to do the dirty dishes. Yes, you get to. Yes, you are able to. There are thousands of people who would love to have the "get to" blessings you have when you stop and realize what they imply. You even get to pay your bills. Think about it. You have a job! You have a lawn!

You had food to eat! You had the electricity to use! You already enjoyed the blessings…now be grateful because when you do you will get more blessings. When you don't like your "have to's" get rid of them or change them to "get to's" and "able to's".

I can't. You have heard this many times and it is still true. When using *"I can't"* in reference to something you desire you are pushing it away with your negative energy. Instead say, *"I want to. I am getting better. I am learning. I am practicing. I am…"* Talk about and focus on the completion of the end result you are bringing into your life. Now, as you get more powerful and more positive you will say, *"I can,"* and then make it happen. Be there in your knowing so you can get there. It certainly gets you there faster. In the beginning people get "there" with baby steps….I want, I am getting there…I am.

These are just a few of the negative words, language and habits we are taught to use as we go through life. Society is lying to itself. We are sabotaging our dreams! Remember, *"Sticks and stones may break my bones and negative words can hurt me and possibly kill*

The Silent Killers

me!"

Once again this is going to take determination and practice to change your habits. Make a game of it. Have your friends, co-workers and family get involved. Set up a reward system. The obvious reward is your life is better! Create your own victory dance for every time you catch yourself and break the habit. Me, my victory dance looks like the dance that Snoopy does in the Charlie Brown Christmas cartoon where Snoopy is dancing above the piano when Schroeder is playing. There's a visual for you. Happy feet and flopping ears and a smile as big as can be! Once again mastery starts with your emotions, then choice and accountability.

Life ABSOLUTES

TRUTHS RECAP: $[(e^E)\ T]A$=Outcome
- Gossip and judgment are silent and deadly killers of my life energy.
- "I am" is always followed by a positive statement.
- I am removing the words, *hate, sorry, try, can't* and *"have to"* and all swear words from my vocabulary.
- I love to laugh and have happy positive thoughts.
- I feel only kind thoughts about others.
- _____
  _____
  _____
  _____

CHAPTER 14

VALIDATE ME

SOMEONE PLEASE MAKE ME FEEL IMPORTANT

This is an all too familiar cry of the lost soul. Please validate me! Anyone please!!! Dear readers, hopefully, by now you realize only you can validate yourself. The "you" who is the Life-Force acting within you. When you keep your attention on that which is only good-love in action or that which love has created you will be validated. The joy and happiness you have attracted into your life will validate that you are a good person. You are important to life. You will like how you look! You will know that your career is one of success because you love doing what you do!

Those of you who think your clothes, degrees, money, your home, your career title, your status, your appearance, etc... are going to get you validation from others in life —you are always going to be seeking that which is illusive. No one can validate you. NO person or thing can do that for you. Sure it feels good to receive praise. However, you do not believe you deserve praise, and you will not accept that praise, and you will still keep seeking validation from the outside world. When you yourself validate yourself, the praise is icing on the cake, if you will. I am not saying do not praise people. What I am saying is, do not become dependent upon praise from others for your self-worth! Some of the so-called most outwardly validated people on the planet are miserable!

TRUTH: Until you allow peace within yourself, you will always be seeking the approval of others. Find peace within. The approval of others will be a quick fix and you will hunger again. You will eat and drink from life and still not be satisfied, because it is not what you are truly seeking. You are seeking the love of self. You are seeking the love of your source of life. You are seeking the knowing and experiences of oneness with that which created all. There and only there will you have peace and harmony, joy and happiness and the

Life ABSOLUTES

true feeling of worth—*I like who I am! I am good enough. I like how I look. I am smart enough. I am successful enough. I am*....whatever it is that you want validated. Eventually, you'll move beyond self validation and will focus your attention on the big picture, the self does not matter to a truly "enlightened being" —you are who you are. Period. I AM. Period. It is no longer about the self— it is about the "One." Until then...

Note: This does not mean you do not expand as a person in being even more abundant and successful in the constructive qualities that you have—just the opposite. You will enjoy attracting more success in all avenues of success because you are sharing joy, happiness, your talents and all the wonderful positive attributes that you have from being a person who chooses to be positive!

So, the nose job, the breast implants, the hair plugs, the sucking, the tucking, the fancy cars, fancy clothes, "the keeping up with the Joneses" does not validate you. You can have all the aforementioned, should that be what you truly want, for positive long-term reasons. Otherwise, ask yourself, *"What do I really want? What am I really seeking?"* Unfortunately, a lot of people seek validation through their sexuality. Once again, that is a quick fix that eventually leaves you feeling empty and used. It leaves you feeling lonelier and more worthless because you gave your power away. You allowed another person to say whether or not you are valid as a person. Do you understand? You give your power away to others when you seek validation from others and addictions—that is giving your power away. You are giving your "freedom" away! Learn how to look in the mirror and I say, *"I like that person! I like what that person believes in! I like what that person does every day! I like me. I am worth liking and I am important to the rest of life."* Now, in the beginning you might have complaints about that person you see in the mirror. That is OK. That is why you are reading this book. YOU have the power to change how you feel about that person in the mirror. Once, you start doing that—others will follow in suit. You and you alone are putting out your own press about yourself! Your feelings, your thoughts and your spoken words/actions—life energy flows out and tells the rest of the world how you feel and what you

Validate Me

believe about yourself!

Be the best P.R. person for yourself. Start believing in yourself today, believing in your dreams and taking action.

I have already encouraged you to write your goals and hopefully you have done that already, NO? Perhaps NOW is the time. I am also going to help you write down what your core values are and what you want them to be, and I encourage you to keep them handy as a personal guideline to live your life—regardless of others immoral, decaying, negative demoralizing actions and choices. YOU can stand tall and be a good example of how love in action feels, looks and behaves. You do not <u>have to</u> sell sex to be attractive or successful. You do not <u>have to</u> buy into the advertising of an immoral society. You do not <u>have to</u> watch or listen to immoral movies, TV shows, commercials and music, language or dress. YOU can take a stand once and for all to live a life of joy, happiness, abundance and self-respect. Then you will be validated by the one person who matters—YOURSELF!

TRUTH: The perfect "you" already exists inside you, just waiting to emerge, sometimes yelling, *"Hello!!!!!!!!!!!!!!! I am here. I love you. You will be perfect once you join me"*—when the inner and outer become one—YOU are perfection. Let the outer become one with the inner self who loves perfection. The inner is the voice of the heart and mind in unison of Divine Love in action. The mind is not the intellect. The mind is that which knows all. The mind is that which we access when we get inspired, when we feel and hear our dreams, and when we discover we know something that the outer self thought it did not. The mind is where everything in the invisible is created before it becomes visible. The intellect is that which can gather data of half-truths based on human fears, doubts, lack and limitations. The mind is devoid of all human qualities. The mind is that which is "all knowing." It is God, or the "universal mind of consciousness." As you already know, the "heart" knows all.

Life ABSOLUTES

TRUTHS RECAP: $[(e^E)\ T]A = \text{Outcome}$

- You will always be seeking the approval of others until you feel peace within, until you find peace within, until you allow peace within yourself. Their approval will be a quick fix and you will soon hunger again. You will eat and drink from life and still not be satisfied because it is not what you are truly seeking. You are seeking the love of self. You are seeking the love of your source of life. You are seeking the knowing and experiences of oneness with that which created all. There and only there will you have peace and harmony, joy and happiness and the true feeling of worth—*I like who I am! I am good enough. I like how I look. I am smart enough. I am successful enough. I am....*whatever it is that you want validated. Eventually, it will not matter. In the big picture it does not matter to a truly "enlightened being" —you are who you are. Period. I AM. Period. It is no longer about the self— it is about the "One."
- When the inner and outer become one—YOU are perfection. Let the outer become one with the inner self who loves perfection. The inner is the voice of the heart and mind in unison of Divine Love in action. The mind is not the intellect. The mind is that which knows all.
- _____
- _____

So, to your oneness of heart and mind and self-validation it really is simple: choose love as your only cause of feelings, thoughts and spoken words/actions. You will be happier than you ever thought possible. No more roller coaster ride. Get off the wheel of human pain and enjoy the life of joy and perfection. That is Validation! Let's get you started on the journey of creating core values. I explain core values most likely in a way you have not heard before! You will find my way fascinating, transforming and uplifting.

Chapter 15

QUALITIES OF THE MASTERS

BEING: ALLOWING PERFECTION TO BE

What is a Master? A master is one who has mastery. **Mastery of what?** In this case I am referring to the Laws of Life. **A Master uses his love, power, knowledge and wisdom, which allows mastery—allowing perfection to BE.** Yes, a Master understands that perfection already is. You have perfection flowing through you. Allow it to stay perfect. Not only that, send it forth through conscious command to help others. Send that pure life energy out to all life to bless it. A Master is free from all negative emotions. A Master lives by the law of "Oneness."

Serve only one master—God the creator of all life. Please keep in mind the God I am referring to is not a religion. When a person serves the human desires of fear, doubt, selfishness, greed, lust, judgment, hate, jealousy, impurity, addictions...the negative human habits that only fulfill quick fixes of the human, that person is serving two masters...sometimes God and the human...sometimes only one master—human gratification. And that person is rewarded with lack and limitations, pain and suffering and a feeling of emptiness only God can fill. Thus, eating from the human side of life and never being full. Is that not what society does... constantly eating, searching, buying, longing...never satisfied for very long leaving the human hungrier?!

Real Masters NEVER want. Turn to your source of all life and keep your attention there and you will never want. Now that does not mean I want you to sit in a corner for the rest of life and contemplate or meditate on the source of all life. I mean acknowledge that Life-God is the giver, doer and knower of all. Turn there for answers. Turn there for your supply. Turn there for whatever it is you require in your outer world because that is where everything originates. Now it can come to you through another person or source because life has

Life ABSOLUTES

sent it to you through that vessel.

When you attempt to take it from another part of life through force you will not keep it long. Thou shalt not steal. Do you steal people's dreams, hopes, energy, happiness, health? Are you stealing? Stop and give it back.

The law of allowing perfection to be is the complete and unconditional understanding that Love/God is acting through you at all times…get out of the way! ☺. You were born a genius. You have been in the way of it. You already know everything I am sharing with you—you have just forgotten because of your acceptance of negative emotions. Negative emotions are like clouds over the sun…the sun is always there and eventually the sun burns away the clouds. When you allow yourself to keep your attention on the source of all life, the clouds of lack, limitation, poor health, you fill in the blank….they will be consumed by the higher rate of vibration you are putting out, thus raising you up and out of the vibration of discord-destruction. Remember, your negative emotions are your alert system saying, *"Warning! You are blocking God/Life/Love from coming through!!!"*

Let me break down just a few of the core values/qualities of a master. **First, A Master Sends Love to the Creator of All Life.** Give Life/God credit for every good thing accomplished or gained in your life or avoided in your life.

Gratitude. Second, A Master is Grateful. Remember, I started being grateful for what I had.

> *"Feeling gratitude and not expressing it is like wrapping a present and not giving it."* -William Arthur Ward

TRUTH: I started remembering how to be grateful. When I started being more grateful, I started pulling myself out and pulling myself up. That's when I decided to start teaching this to people in the hopes that all of mankind would stop self-destructing.

Qualities of The Masters

Compassion. Third, A Master is Compassionate. When you're seeing people, you want to make sure that you're seeing them in a light where you can help them or you can have compassion. You have compassion for those people because they're on a journey in life just like you are. You're figuring it out every day. You're remembering how to be better at what you do every single day. You're working on your perfection every single day, so it's better when you look to find the good in people. If you look to find the good in people you're putting out positive emotions. You're putting out positive thoughts about them. They don't even know it; you're making them feel better just because you're putting out positive thoughts and positive emotions about them. You're uplifting them without them even knowing that you're doing it, because you're putting energy out towards them that's positive.

And when you do that what happens? You get more positive energy back. You are allowing perfection to "Be," so you can help other people get their focus back on what's positive. You're doing them a service. And you're also doing yourself a service. Because what happens is, when you start choosing to be in that place of *"what would love do here, what is positive here, what's compassionate here, what's forgiveness here,"* your world becomes full of people who are just like you. The old saying, *"Birds of a feather flock together,"* is true. You're attracting more and more positive people into your world, by choosing to be positive, by choosing to be in a place of love, loving you, loving other people.

Praise. Fourth, A Master is Praiseful. Now, you're giving praise, *"Oh, Sally that was really good. You did a good job today. You know, you were really on. You know, my wife did this really great thing today. My parents are wonderful and terrific. They did this..."* When you're giving praise, that's not judging in a negative way. That is pointing out the good qualities in people.

Usually when you're judging somebody it's because you want praise, or you are lacking in praise. So give yourself praise. Stop and give yourself praise. I know that sounds odd, praise yourself then you will feel worthy. You don't think that you're worthy of praise?

Life ABSOLUTES

You refuse to give yourself praise? How is anybody else going to give you praise? They might give you praise, but you know what? You probably won't hear it and or accept it.

So start praising yourself today—every day. Perhaps you start with giving yourself praise five times a day. Build up to 10. Build up to 20. While you're at it, give someone else 10! Give 10 praises to other people. Give yourself 20, then give 20 to other people. Give yourself 30, then give 30 to other people. Kind of sounds silly, but it becomes very fun. It becomes very fun because it gets you in such a place of positive energy, of positive outcomes happening in your life. I love doing this when I go to the grocery store, post office, bank, gas station… obviously the "work place" and at home!!! Find your so-called enemy and give them praise!!! You will experience miracles.

Forgiveness: Fifth, A Master is Forgiving. Forgive yourself and others. Until you forgive yourself you will not allow others to forgive you. Until you forgive others you will have placed yourself in an emotional jail.

TRUTH: People who have gone on national TV saying they have forgiven a killer are setting themselves free! They are not condoning the act of the human who killed. They are realizing that the human was in pain. In TRUTH God does exist within the flesh body. We are asked to love our "enemies," we then love God. When you hate your enemy, you then hate God. When you choose to not forgive, you are imprisoned by your hate for the rest of your life. The killer might have found God and asked for forgiveness and it is up to God-Life to handle that life stream. So that person might be living in peace and remembering the truth of life while you are in a living hell of hate and pain and missing out on all the blessings life has to offer you. So forgiveness is two-fold. Remember you love the life energy in them that is God not the human! This principle is an ideal basis for all relationships. There are many more Master qualities later in this section. So you ask…

How do I return to the place of mastery? Everyone wants to. Let me

Qualities of The Masters

start from this approach. Humans run around learning by going to school, college, universities, reading books... basically by studying. Great. Learned information is worthless when unused. It is like having a life raft that would save your life and you say, *"No, it takes too much effort to get in it and then what will I do once I'm in it?"* So you opt to drown instead. Are you drowning? Why would you do that? Seems silly, yes? Well, that is what people do all day long. You have learned information, some of you have applied it for a while and gained knowledge, and yet you do not use it for one reason or another all the time. Why? Whatever the reasons, they are ALL excuses. Most people do not use their knowledge because they have not formed the habit. Or better yet, the old "bad" habit is easier. Then they continue to moan and groan that life is not fair—*"if I only knew how to do this or that or had this opportunity or that chance like so and so."*

Well, perhaps "so and so" took their knowledge (now, I am talking about constructive knowledge) and applied it, used it on a regular basis, gaining wisdom and applied that wisdom on a regular basis and now has mastery. Mastery comes from actually applying and using the learned information, then it <u>then</u> becomes knowledge, and then becomes wisdom. Wisdom coupled with love and power create mastery. Love, wisdom and power, these three divine elements create mastery. Most people are lacking wisdom the most.

Most people require more discipline to apply their new knowledge on a minute to minute, hourly, daily, weekly basis...you get the idea. It takes discipline, determination, dedication and desire. Apply this truth for 40 days and prove me wrong.

You will gain more wisdom...from that wisdom you will have more mastery, from that mastery you will gain more learning and knowledge. The process I just described has an incredible momentum. Did I mention constructive mastery allows success to flow in? Abundantly flow in. Eventually allowing perfection to BE! The only reason the human does not take action to apply their new knowledge is fear. Fear of not knowing what will happen next, fear of leaving behind the old and familiar...even though it is a lacking

Life ABSOLUTES

and a painfully unfulfilling life! What i̲f̲????????? OHHHHHHH…
So many people say they have read hundreds of books on being spiritual. I say great. When are you going to be masterful and allow perfection to be in your life? What are you waiting for? The usual response is, *"Well, I have one more book to read. I don't know where to start. I tried and it wasn't fun."* These are the excuses of the ego. All excuses! Right NOW, apply the information in this book, gain knowledge for 40 days—set the momentum, get in your airplane and fly higher, live in the State of Success while living in the City of Success!

Really live these principles for 40 days, then you will have your proof one way or another. Granted you might not have read the right books prior to this one. What I am sharing with you came to me from crying out that night when I demanded God to help me. That was the human letting go and saying, *"I will serve only one master."* Then the sun shone bright and started burning off the clouds of my despair. My willingness to return home burned off the clouds, and it still gets brighter every day. At that moment I remembered God answers my every call. It is up to me to listen and be aware. Life-God gives me everything constructive that I ask for. When I do not have it, it is not God's fault…it is mine and no one else's!

Assignment: Find people who have the qualities you like and would like to posses and start having those qualities too, emulate them. Yes, start owning them. Be them. Live them. Share them. Embody them. Be a living example of God in action. You say, *"Excuse me, that does not sound like much fun!"* The fun you think you are having now is short term. Being God in action, love in action, and good in action is eternal. Only God is everlasting perfection. When all is said and done, how you touch the hearts of your fellow man is all people really remember—that is an outcome of mastery.

Here is your assignment. <u>Write down all the qualities you believe make you a pure, perfect being of The Creator.</u> Write them down. This is YOUR Core Value List. Now be them! YES. Be them. Allow them to exist in you every waking moment. Be conscience of your choices. Focus on the qualities, traits, skills, and behaviors that you

Qualities of The Masters

have every waking moment. Stop being a pinball in the experience called life. Be in charge. You want so-called control in your life then "BE" masterful. You know what is expected of you from Life. Stop making excuses. When you stop, you will truly enjoy the abundance life has and always has had for you. It is up to you to gain the mastery that takes you into the existence of your abundance and joy. The choice is yours and always has been.

Right now humans are very masterful at what they do not want!!! Here are a few suggestions for your list, to help those of you who require a little assistance. Of course all of these masterful qualities are sub-qualities of Divine Love-God. Loving, joyful, forgiving, compassionate, happy, pure, hopeful, faithful, giving, peaceful, harmonious, graceful, accepting, appreciative, inspired, radiant, alive, funny, playful, bless yourself and others, sincere, loyal, integrity, honest, encouraging, supportive, prompt, courteous, perfect, divine, humble, beautiful, elegant, respectful, virtuous, transcendent, powerful, unwavering, fearless, obedient, courageous, innocent, all-knowing, oneness, silent, doer, free, musical, young, youthful, creative, helpful, uplifting, caring, healer, dedicated, disciplined, determined, focused, worthy, patient, honorable, gracious, kind, wise ...a few suggestions to get you started.

So how do you transform yourself with the list I just gave you? Start acknowledging that these qualities exist inside of you already! Acknowledge every time you embody one or more of those qualities. Read the list in the nature that you say, *"I am___,"* saying with a feeling of belief that you are those qualities. Read my list or your list with acceptance and joy. Breathe your qualities in. Own them—this is what actors do. Good actors embody the qualities of the role they perform to the extent of being the qualities of the character and allowing the qualities of the character to be in charge...letting those qualities take over their own qualities. This is also known as "getting rid of old habits." We all know you can only get "rid of" an old habit by replacing it with new habit. How about good ones that have been around for eternity and proven winners?

That is what you want to BE. Be God qualities. In order to "be"

Life ABSOLUTES

them, put your attention on them by feeling them, and seeing them in yourself. See your human transformed into them. Flood your senses with those POWERFUL, masterful qualities...allow them to take over the human...in other words raise the human up into perfection—mastery. Sure the human is arguing that this is too much work. In reality it is effortless to be perfect...it is the conflict of the human causing the effort. The struggle of the human fighting to not Let GO! Let go of the EGO. **How do you let go? Take your emotional attention off of whatever it is you want to release! It is that simple.**

You will then be in this world but not of it. You embody the above masterful qualities and any other constructive ones you have added. Life will be heaven here on earth for you!

Quick note, avoid attempting to impress people, because that is just allowing the EGO to be in charge. Dress, talk, walk and live to be one with the source because you are a vessel that glorifies life. Choose to look, feel and act your best at all times because you can and want to show the rest of the world God is good. All other reasons are for gratification of the human.

As the line in the movie, "The Matrix" says, *"There is a difference between knowing the path and walking the path."* The door is open from heaven's side—the treasure house of life— at all times. Is today the day you will open it and leave it open?

Be masterful. Be YOUR true God self! You know the truth in your inner being. Listen to it. Follow it. Apply it. Be it. Allow it.

Example: I teach actors. Johnny wants to be good at auditioning. Then Johnny must apply the knowledge he has learned. Apply it, live those qualities, be those qualities, allow those skills to be perfect. Fear stops perfection. Fear, doubt and selfishness are all impure. That's it. Nothing else. They keep you and "all the Johnny's" of the world from perfection. Right about now you might be saying what about......? Ask yourself, where does that stem from? Fear? Doubt? Selfishness? Impurity?

Qualities of The Masters

When someone says, *"I need fear to tell me something isn't safe"*—yes you do until you gain the wisdom to know when something is not safe. Example: Jumping off the Empire State Building with no equipment to keep you safe. YES, you should be afraid. The fear is telling you, *let's think about this choice.* Is your fear valid? YES. You would be jumping to your death. Let's make a masterful choice instead. Now fear of someone laughing at you in an audition or not being hired for a job—is that fear valid? No, you will not die. Well, to date there are no recorded accounts of an actor dying from not getting a job or making a mistake in an audition. The fear is ego-based. The fear is based on you giving your power to another person—giving another person's opinion power over you.

The more Johnny applies his knowledge of how a professional actor auditions, the better he will become. His confidence will increase and wisdom will be gained. Eventually, the process of knowledge, wisdom and mastery will take him to the place of not caring about whether he gets the job or even whether the casting director, producer or director likes him. Johnny will enjoy the process because he is doing what he loves to do with his life. He will be blessing everyone he comes in contact with, thus, helping his fellow man!

The truth is, maybe Johnny wasn't supposed to get the job. The whole picture is always bigger than you and simpler than all that. You are here to uplift and inspire other humans to be masterful and allow perfection to be in their lives too. Be the example of mastery and allowing perfection to be.

A wonderful story was shared with me that went something like this…this is true. This young lady wanted to be a spiritual leader so she signed up with one of the organizations that allowed her to go to a less fortunate area of the world. She ended up going to South America. Everyday she taught the villagers about God. Well, the TRUTH of the matter is, she was not very good at it…not gifted at it…so it seemed. Everyday, for several years she taught and taught…nothing really ever came about from it. She finally returned home. Years later in the same village this huge spiritual growth happened. People were following this young man who was a

Life ABSOLUTES

powerful, gifted spiritual leader. He had done amazing things in his village and the surrounding ones. When asked what had inspired him, he said, *"There was this lady who taught us every day, she was not good at all and yet, she kept at it. Her dedication, determination, passion and discipline to this truth made me want to know why she so loved what she did and why she wanted to share this truth."*

TRUTHS RECAP: $[(e^E) \; T]A = Outcome$

- How do I let go? I take my emotional attention off of whatever it is I what to release! It is that simple.
- **Reminder:** My assignment. Write down all the qualities I believe make me a pure, perfect being of The Creator. I choose to be them! YES. Be them. Allowing them to exist in me every waking moment. I am conscious of my choices. I am focused on the qualities, traits, skills, and behaviors that I have every waking moment. The choice is mine and always has been.
- The door is open from heaven's side at all times. Today is the day I open it and leave it open! Negative emotions close the door.

So, be masterful. Apply all the knowledge you have been given. People say, *"Well, if I just knew what to do next after this I would start."* Well, when you do what you have been given the knowledge to do, you will be given more knowledge through the wisdom and mastery gained from the first knowledge. Remember, I talked about this in the goal setting, achieving chapter. Stop making excuses. Apply your knowledge and the wisdom and mastery will come—you will allow perfection to be. You know the truth in your inner being. Listen to it. Follow it. Apply it. Use it. Allow it. Be it.

CHAPTER 16

THE FACTOR OF ONE

YOUR RELATIONSHIP WITH THE ONE

Your relationships are the foundation of your joy and abundance: Career, health and finances...thus, making relationship the Factor of the "one".

On the highest level of relationship is your relationship with that which created all and gives you life. No not your parents. I call that life energy "God." For the sake of conversation I will use the name God.

God is the key, number "one" relationship you must have in your life. God must come first and foremost. All love and adoration must go to the source of all happiness—God.

As human beings we have a tendency to give credit to the human, to our parents, to our spouse, to our lover, to our children, to our bosses, to our clothes, to our money, to our careers, to everything but God. Let me repeat. God must come first. Go back to the formula. Love everything with divine love. When you love everything through divine love you love God. To truly be powerful and successful, acknowledge that all good has come through God, your life energy.

TRUTH: God uses human beings as vessels. God works through every person around you. Now, it might not appear that way to you, however, God is the only source that supplies life...therefore on some level God is working through every single person.

Not only through people but through nature. Yes, it is true. One should bless and be grateful for the food we eat and drink; the sun, the wind, the rain, the earth and yes, fire too.

Life ABSOLUTES

On the simplest level all life came from that one source and has been misused or blessed. When that which you see is destructive then bless it and ask it to be set free from its negative energy and or creation. Mankind creates destructive creations not God. Mankind misuses life. God does not. Please take the time to contemplate this and be more grateful for the billions of blessing you have received in this lifetime and perhaps have misused or wasted! That was your energy you misused and now it might be in your life as lack and limitation. Have you misused money in the past? Misused food, alcohol, drugs, sex and power?

Have you misused the earth, polluted the air, set fire to things you should not have? Have you been ungrateful for the beauty of nature? Ungrateful for the beauty of the rain that provides you shelter by the trees it grows? Have you been ungrateful for the sun that grows the crops that feed you? Have you been ungrateful for the fuel, electricity, and the clothes you wear? Yes, these all factor into your relationship with life. The source of all abundance.

One must be grateful. This is the true understanding of minimalism. A minimalist understands everything in existence is theirs to enjoy. Everything is a gift from Life-God. All of these are what humans call miracles. To God they are every-day gifts. Do you realize that a plant uses a year's energy to give you an apple to eat, that you perhaps consume in a minute, or even worse, throw away just because you can.

So that 1930's saying, *"Eat all your food because there are children in China starving,"* perhaps should be, *"Bless all of your food and waste not, because that is your life energy. Use it wisely and it will return to you a lifetime of abundant harvest. Abuse it, take it for granted and you will have a harvest of drought and scarcity—lack and limitation."*

Let's take this to the human level. Do you abuse your personal relationships? Do you take people for granted? Do you treat them poorly by judging, condemning, gossiping about them, ignoring them and just flat out attempting to control them? One cannot treat any

The Factor of One

part of life with disrespect and expect life to treat you differently in return. What you put out is what you get back! Positive returns positive and negative returns negative.

Now, you can correct your past mistakes. You can apologize. You can ask for forgiveness. You can bless all the people and that which you treated poorly in the past.

You can pour forth-Divine Love into all those whom you have wronged in the past. Pour forth Divine-Love and ask that they be blessed greater than they can imagine. You can forgive all of those who have wronged you thus, gaining your freedom. You can, as of today, start being grateful for all of life. For all relationships and the blessings they bring into your life. Yes, they are blessing you in some way, shape or form. If for no other reason than to give you the opportunity to make right the energy you misused in your past.

Perhaps it is the "hello" moment and you just silently bless that life and ask that it be blessed with greater happiness. Perhaps the person or thing is a reminder that you are to be grateful for all the minute blessings in your life. Perhaps it is a reminder that in the past you made mistakes and now this person deserves forgiveness. Remember, whatever you put out you get back.

I have talked about relationships early in the book. No one has the right to control another person's life. We all have freedom of choice whether you like it or not. Yes, there are consequences to everyone's choices/actions. They are accountable for them. As a fellow human we can advise. That does not mean manipulate others and use our power to intimidate others.

Marriage—simple and to the point.

TRUTH: You are friends first and foremost. Not lovers. Get rid of that idea. A lover is a toy of which you tire and give away or put in the closet and forget. A relationship should never be based on sexual attraction…yeah, I know…that is how almost every relationship starts—sexual attraction and that is why so few last and end so violently and on such a negative note. Some people believe that sexual energy should be used only for procreation so they choose to be celibate. Of course it is your choice how you use any and all of your energy

Humans have the ability to think and reason. Stop acting like animals. Marriage is a relationship between two friends. Two people acknowledging that their friendship is one that they want to last forever, and acknowledging that it can sustain the biggest storms that come along. Not only that, should we decide to have children, we must have love pure enough to share with them, provide good life values for them, and nurture them. Plus, we should provide emotional, spiritual and mental support.

Note: True friends can have a disagreement and then make up and laugh about it. **Then why do married couples have such problems? They were never true friends.** They were sexual partners. *"What if we were virgins when we got married?"* you say. You were virgins and you were sexual partners in energy thoughts, and an agreement to wait did not stop the exchanges of animal sexual attraction. Love that is real does not require a sexual relationship to validate it. So many troubled relationships have used sex as a bargaining, manipulating tool. Instead of using open honest conversation like real friends. Sex gets used to fill the voids. Then the arguments happen, the sex is withdrawn and like a wild animal the one doing the withholding has the power over the other one. I have already talked about using power over another person. It only creates more negative reactions and the outcome—slowly or quite quickly the relationship falls apart.

Another factor that creates the start of an unstable marriage-relationship is one based on career. Both people are workaholics. At first that is great. Very little time is required to sustain the relationship. Both parties are OK with a minimal amount of time being spent together as long as some quality time is shared. Do you see the writing on the wall on this one? One person is going to disagree how much time is really quality time. What happens when one person's career shifts? Downsizes? The energy is subtle or

The Factor of One

dynamic and unless there was truly a solid friendship in place...once again the relationship has to adapt or it falls apart.

So, what is a good friendship? Remember the master qualities? Trust, loyalty, honesty, caring, compassionate, loving in a non-romantic way, forgiving, understanding, flexible, good listener, good communicator, honest, loyal, hardworking, dependable, friendly, caring, sharing, compassionate, forgiving, understanding, on-time, funny, accepting, faithful and many more. Plus, each person must be healthy emotionally. That means the other person is just fine being by themselves. They do not require someone to complete them. Forget the line, *"You complete me." "Buzz,"* wrong! God completes YOU! God gives you the love you require. God gives you the joy and happiness you require. God gives you the supply you require. Well, then why do I want a spouse or significant other when God "completes" me? LOL, good question...a relationship is about sharing the gifts God gives you with that special person. About expanding the gifts God gives you. About using the gifts God has given you. No, you do not <u>have to</u> be married to do that! However, throughout the centuries the ceremony has survived and it gives a special joy and happiness that other relationships do not offer—as long as the relationship is always coming from a place of respect and friendship. It also gives support, protection and nurturing to the woman and children—family members sharing in nurturing each other.

Why does a piece of paper a marriage license give a person a right to dominate another person? It does not! Why does a marriage license make couples think that other person should be perfect? Why does that piece of paper make people think the other person should be at their beck and call? Why does that piece of paper give a person the right to abuse another person physically, emotionally or financially? It does NOT!!! It is a lie, a lie that married couples use to be dishonest and live in negative energy. It is an excuse to abuse another life! Marriage is not a license to live in negative energy! Married people obey the laws of energy just like single people—surprise.

Life ABSOLUTES

Now, why is it harder to stay positive when you are married—because you are living day in and day out in another person's energy. You are susceptible to their negative emotions. You are required to stay positive no matter what the spouse it doing. That is why you better be best friends before you get married or you better get busy becoming best friends. That means letting water roll off your back like a duck at times. That means having the communications skills of a top CEO. That means having the best listening skills of a friend. That means having the patience of a "saint." That means forgiving, being compassionate, laughing, joking, compromising, caring, sharing, enjoying time alone, dedicating quality time to communicating your feelings, dreams, so-called fears (you can go back and read the Qualities of the Masters). It also means to be understanding and willing to let a person go.

Yes, sometimes you must let a person go. Sometimes one person shifts so dynamically into the positive or the negative that the relationship is too different...*birds of a feather flock together*. It is usually the person who shifts upward in energy, the person who gets more positive, who wants to leave. The person who is negative wants to stay in the relationship and feed off the energy of the positive person. They become like a vampire sucking the life out of the other person should that person not move on. Or you end up with two people living two separate lives under the same roof and having incomplete lives because they are living a lie and settling for less or worse yet, living in the City of Abandon Dreams.

I could go on for a whole book on partner relationships. Follow the formula I put forth at the beginning of this book—it always works.

As far as relationships with family and co-workers and others—the same principles apply! Go figure.

Be a good person to all people. Listen, care, be forgiving, respectful, grateful for them, acknowledge them, care about them, share with them, love them (not sexually), nurture them, uplift them, inspire them, praise them...you get the picture. All the positive qualities you like to receive and enjoy. Remember, the only being a good person

The Factor of One

serves is God. With all others we share our gifts of love, talent, time and money. In reality you are giving back to the God life inside that person, place, nature or condition.

After applying the aforementioned, and finding that the relationship is still not working—move on. Let it go. Bless it! And move on. Perhaps in the future it will come back around and the energy will have shifted. The only way you can stay in the place of a healthy relationship is to understand sometimes the best choice is to love the person silently, bless them and move on. Note, I said *healthy*...not being a stalker or pining away hoping one day "they" will love me too. That is not healthy.

So once you start establishing healthy, positive relationships in your life your career will flourish more. All careers operate around other individuals—even when they exist via email and through telecommunications. You are still connected through energy-emotions, thoughts and actions.

TRUTH: Your career relationships require the same interpersonal skills as your personal relationships. They are just now called professional skills. Life really is simple; the rules do not change, just the environment and the so-called players.

Business skills: Trustworthy, loyal, honest, caring, compassionate, loving in a non-romantic way, forgiving, understanding, flexible, good listener, good communicator, hardworking, dependable, friendly, sharing, on-time, each person must be healthy emotionally. That means the other person is just fine being able to work alone. Be a team player, fun, upbeat, positive, sensitive, reliable, skilled, likeable, personable...once again you get the picture. You are a being in relationship with life 100% of the time—there is no escaping life. No, not even through so-called death are you taken out of life. That which gave your flesh life still exists, just not in the flesh form. Life does not die. The flesh dies.

You are now living a life of positive personal relationships, professional relationships and now here comes your health. This is

Life ABSOLUTES

simple too. Your flesh is kept alive by the energy called life. You are now using your life energy positively and or qualifying your life energy with constructive emotions, therefore, the cells of the body are being charged with the pure energy of Divine Love. Your flesh stays healthy from the standpoint of your emotional body. Laughter is the best medicine…Divine Love is the best preventative medicine.

Now it is up to you to exercise and put healthy food into that body: food that does not poison the cells and cause them to die. Granted there are thousands of books on the topic of eating healthily. I will touch on the topics not so widely talked about and those are meat, alcohol and drugs.

Well, **"drugs"** is obvious. Drugs alter the mind and therefore the energy of the body causing the rate of vibration—the energy of your body—to vibrate at a lower rate. They alter the natural harmonious, vibration of the body. The lower the rate of vibration, the closer to death your body comes…thus, drug over-doses.

Drinking Alcohol is a legal and acceptable form of socializing and has been touted as giving good health. Well, truth be told, that which makes the body healthier in the wine is in grape juice too. Drink the grape juice. Yes, even when you drink only a glass of wine you are altering the rate of vibration of your energy. Alcohol lowers the rate of vibration in your body, thus, lowering your resistance to negative energy, negative emotions, negative thoughts and negative words-actions. The human becomes more vulnerable to negative suggestion from other people when consuming alcohol because of the lower resistance. Remember the story about drinks after work and how people eventually end up gossiping and judging other people for so-called fun? Alcohol invites in all the negative energy that exists in the environment of where you are at the time you are drinking, and up until the point at which the alcohol leaves the cells of your body. By the time the alcohol has left your body, your rate of vibration has been lowered not only by the alcohol but by the negative emotions you experienced and by the negative energy to which you were exposed while "under the influence." Now say your human is arguing right about now, that's because it is that child like behavior

The Factor of One

of the human ego throwing a temper tantrum because it can't have its own way. It's seeking the quick fix.

Ask yourself, what are you going to miss when you stop drinking? What? Whatever your answer was, you only think you will miss out on those things…it is a lie.

Or perhaps the answers you mentioned are not positive and alcohol is a good scapegoat? Alcohol gives you nothing that you cannot live happily ever after without. Go 40 days without it. Now, if you cannot go 40 days, then you know there is a problem. When you do go 40 days you will realize the conversations over alcohol always ended up going into the negative. People's emotions go to the negative. Words get said that cause regret. Actions are taken that cannot be undone. Give it a shot. No pun intended. Go without alcohol for 40 days and be honest with yourself. You have better relationships without it. Those who say otherwise are lying to themselves. Hopefully, you will realize this truth.

Meat is loaded with negative energy. Why? The animal, fish, crustaceans, bird felt pain when it was killed. That energy of pain registers in the meat of the animal and you are ingesting it as "energy" to feed your body. How can your body be healthy when you're feeding it negative energy? Yes, I hear all the high protein eaters of the world. Read on. There are pro athletes who are vegetarians—Olympians who are vegetarians. Now, you are saying, *"I don't feel good when I stop eating meat."* That is because your body is going through withdrawals from not having negative energy. The ego wants you to stay in that negative place. When you stop eating "meat" your body is going through withdrawals from the chemicals in the meat, and you are now detoxifying the chemicals you have accumulated over the years just like a drug addict or alcoholic. Your body is operating at a lower rate of vibration as a direct result of ingesting the meat, alcohol and/or drugs. Most people have read or heard about the body going through withdrawals. For some people you might feel fine in a day, for others it could take months. However, YOU will feel better once the body has shifted and healed itself. FREE at last from not only the chemicals, also

Life ABSOLUTES

the negative energy that was "silently" sabotaging you! Notice when you are stressed out—you want a drink, a smoke or a big steak? That is because your body is addicted to negative energy!!! Remember, negative energy can give you a false high—the quick fix. The aforementioned are prime examples of the quick fix!!! As always it is your choice how to use your life energy.

Last on the list is financial supply, your wealth. Why is "it" last, when it is what seems to be the biggest driving factor as to why people get out of bed in the morning? Why? Because let's revisit the million dollar question... *"What is your purpose in life?"* Answer: To be love in action! Well, you are NOW love in action in your relationships, you are NOW love in action in your career, therefore, your health is almost taking care of itself because you have been filling it with loving emotions, and thoughts. The body has also been doing loving activities, so the last factor is financial supply. At this point the formula is still the same. What is money but energy! Money is energy. What are gold, silver, diamonds? They are elements of the, earth, water, air and fire—nature—life's energy. So you have blessed life and used life positively through your relationships, career and health...you are a magnet right? You attract what you put out right? You get what you put your attention on right? YES!!!

For the sake of a positive outcome I will run the formula with positive choices....

I am positive in my relationships, positive in my career, positive with my health...I am one big positively charged magnet that can only attract....you got it—financial supply!!! As long as you love money and are grateful for it you will attract it.

Now, at any time should you put negatives into the formula lack will start appearing. I hear the question coming. What about all those "bad" people who have lots of money? Well, notice how their lives end. Notice their health. Notice their relationships. The reason they have money is because they have no fear about it. They are positive about money and everything about it.

The Factor of One

When you have negative emotions about anything in life you receive what you do not want: being fat or broke. Or you do not get what you want: i.e.: Being fit or having lots of money. You attract what you do not want because that is where **you're** putting your attention-energy: on those bad relationships, poor health, being unemployed, having a low paying job, or poor grades in school. When you want something from a place of lack, you are chasing it, grabbing at it, holding on so tight to that which you do have. Example: the relationship you cannot have, the money you wish you had. When you feel and say you are broke, you attract more of that into your life. When you only see lack in your life that is all you get. **When you are NOT grateful for what you have and are not willing to share it, you end up with less.**

The law of attraction does not change with the personality of the person. You might say that is not fair. *"That person is kind and thoughtful and so giving."* Well, they are most likely afraid of being poor, afraid of being without and perhaps in the debt. Perhaps they are pretending to be happy and pretending to give, when in reality they are doing all of the "kindness" to receive a reward. One must give freely without expecting reward. Yes, even doing your so-called job. Do it because you love to! Then the paycheck is rewarding! Pay your monthly bills with a heart of gratitude that you have electricity, you have water, you have a car, you have a roof over your head. Be grateful. Think of it this way too, you are employing people when you pay your bills. You must be willing to circulate your life energy in a positive giving, sharing, loving, uplifting manner and then life will return it to you. This does not mean spending what you do not have for a quick fix high.

So, the so-called "bad" person enjoys how they earn or receive their money. Remember, when it is a quick fix there is a price to pay! And those so-called "bad" people including "Dream Stealers" always get their just reward.

Now, can you have supply and have poor health? Sure. Can you have a good marriage and no money? Sure. However, look at the people who have an unbalanced life. The other elements eventually start to

Life ABSOLUTES

decay and the house of cards comes falling down when any of the four elements are left to the negative way of life or out of balance with life.

The formula of "one" is based on the easiest and simplest way to keep balance and abundance in check. Feel free to get there however you choose. I like the simple way with the least amount of resistance!

This way your "house" is built of the strongest stones and mortar on the most solid ground above the turmoil of the other world's chaos. Remember, God/Life first and foremost and abundance is a given….that is "The Factor of One." Your relationship with God is the foundation that will withstand anything that comes at your career, health and finances because it is the life energy that provides all of that to you.

Is there an appearance of lack in your life? Then you have turned away from your source through negative energy and turned off your own faucet on God's abundance. Turn around, God's abundance has not gone anywhere. Turn back to positive emotions, thoughts and actions and the door to your supply house—your treasure house will fly open. Remember, be patient…ask for forgiveness from yourself, then give forgiveness to others. Bless all who have wronged you and bless all those you have wronged. Every time you do, more joy, happiness, peace and harmony will flood into your life and bring abundance in more ways than money can into your life. BE AWARE…do not get all cocky and forget where it came from and start misusing it again. Keep your heart pure, your mind pure and your body pure…then you will have perfection in your life.

What do these four elements teach us? What are the lessons?

TRUTHS RECAP: $[(e^E)\ T]A=Outcome$

- **Relationships** teach YOU the formula of life, what you sow you reap, ask and thy shall receive, see with only one eye, love thy neighbor as thyself, do unto others as you would

The Factor of One

have others do unto you—*accountability*—I am *creating* the world I live in. **Career** shows me the importance of sharing my gifts-talents—*fulfilling my purpose in life*. **Health** teaches me to honor my higher self—that *my body is indeed a temple of the living God*. **Finance** teaches me to *let go—all belongs to God*/Life.

- All four elements require the human to remember the formula and live by it while *allowing the human to return back to the source of perfection—the "One" —thus allowing mastery to return to the self.*

- _____
  _____
- _____
  _____

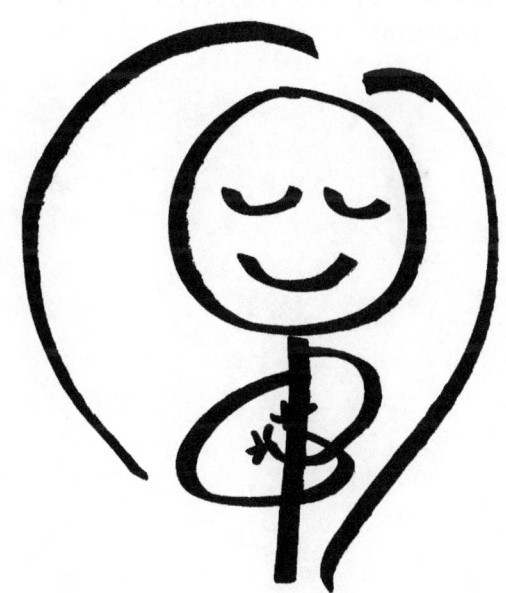

Is today the day you will stop making excuses and return to your source and love and obey it?   Image 48

Life ABSOLUTES

"Things are going really good and again I would like to thank you for your help. I have been able to put the tools that you taught me to work in so many different situations and it always keeps me moving in the right direction. I started a new company two months ago so I could get my auto dealer's license and it has taken two months to get everything together but I should be receiving my actual license next week. Work is good too I have changed the energy in the shop and with my customers and now we are always busy. Thank you so much for sharing with me your wonderful insight on living and loving life. I woke up before my alarm went off today for the first time in months. As my morning goes on things just keep getting clearer and clearer.

*Decisions and actions I have taken in the past now make perfect sense why they failed. I feel as if somebody just handed me an **"easy button"** for life."* -Shane Glasgow, Business Owner

Write down what your choices are. NOW! What are the new positive choices you want for your life?

CHAPTER 17

COLORS AND MORE

CONSTRUCTIVE OR DESTRUCTIVE

Let's talk about the rate of vibration colors have. Colors are made up of life energy since life energy was used to make whatever the item is that the colors are in or placed upon. Each color has a rate of vibration that makes its quality special. The rate of vibration is focused on the optic nerve of the eye and also comes in through the emotional body, whether seen or not, thus effecting you and those around you.

Let's talk about the constructive colors: white, pink, gold/yellow, blue, violet and green. All of these colors have divine qualities. All other colors are destructive I will get to them later.

Let's start with white. **White** contains all colors. Think of light not pigments. White is the highest rate of vibration a color can be. White has the emotional messaging of all the colors: perfection, purity, illumination, it heals and it offers protection.

Pink is the color of Divine Love, which is compassion and forgiveness.

Gold/yellow is the vibratory rate of peace. Gold is soothing and uplifting, it harmonizes the being into higher knowledge.

Blue is power, thus the power suit. Wear blue wisely misused power is very destructive. Blue also energizes a person and gives them strength.

Green is the vibratory rate that attracts money and supply when used constructively.

Violet is known in the natural medicine circles and by spiritualist to

Life ABSOLUTES

heal and purify.

Now the aforementioned colors have more constructive qualities then the few I mentioned, however, the aforementioned will be most helpful to get you started. Those colors can also be pale, pastel or richer in color and still be constructive.

Destructive colors are black, red and all muddy, muted and or altered colors. OK. I hear some people from the fashion world and the advertising industry screaming right about now.

Let's be honest. What did the color **BLACK** portray for centuries? DEATH. That's right. DEATH—devoid of all life. Evil spirits and the forces of darkness. Is that the energy or non-energy you want to be wearing and have surrounding you? Do you want to knowingly suck the life out of your life stream? Do you want to intentionally shut off your life stream of positive energy flow? It is up to you. OK. I took art classes…black pigment is the absorption of all colors. We are talking about light. Light is energy in its purest form. Black is devoid of light. And the night is not black…it is dark blue… powerful universe we live in!

Red, what does red mean? Anger, fear, warning!!! Think about how red is used, traffic lights and stops signs to warn us! Be Afraid-danger! Fast food restaurants use red to stimulate the emotions of anger, fear, frustration so you "super-size" or order more than you want to pacify your emotions and then LEAVE—*we want to make room for more 'angry people.'* Why do little children cry when they see Santa Clause? The red bothers their sensitive emotions!

I know this for a TRUTH, before I was aware of the red factor; I had a red baseball cap. Every time I wore it to my friend's house, her child would start screaming…then when I took the cap off and put it out of sight he stopped…instantly!

Why, are people drawn to black and red…the quick fix. Black is thought of as "elegant," classy, you become more refined. Wrong, you have less energy in TRUTH! That is what you think feels like

Colors And More

refined. You put on more make-up in order to wear black because you look like "death warmed over." You want to look sophisticated?

Wear Royal Purple...there is a reason it is called royal and there is also Royal Blue...both very slenderizing and uplifting to the soul and regal. Wear white and gold. There is class, style and sophistication!

Browns, grays and dirty colors are just that...dirty. They have been tainted with black or red or altered forms of energy that are low in vibration. Creams and off-whites are acceptable ☺.

Quick note: **Microwaves** use lower rates of energy. Go online and look at a chart of "the spectrum of light." A microwave's energy alters the rate of vibration in your food to lessen its energy output...thus, killing the life source in it. So you are eating a lot of empty calories with no "life" energy in them. Your body requires life. The higher the vibration, the happier, healthier, more productive and truly successful you will be. And yes, **infrared** is damaging—it's used in the medical industry especially in the beauty world. Red is red. Look on the chart. It has a lower vibration rate than "visible light." It causes a quick fix and then your emotional body has to deal with the consequences!

TRUTH: The bottom line, all life has vibration. You choose what you want to do with "life" and deal with the consequences. I am giving you this information to test it out! Sure I ended up in the beginning getting rid of half my clothes—well worth it! Sure I quit eating meaty flesh and consuming alcohol...not because I had to, because I "discovered" the truth and I choose to walk the walk of positive energy. Some even say I look younger SINCE MAKING THESE CHANGES. I accept that!

TRUTHS RECAP: $[(e^E)$ T$]$A=Outcome

- I choose to wear positive colors on my body and surround myself with positive colors.
- _____

Life ABSOLUTES
- _____
- _____

CHAPTER 18

ATTRACTING ABUNDANCE

YOU ARE A MAGNET

The biggest "quick fix" that our society bought into is being addicted to money. We've been motivated by the thought, *let's make a lot of money! Let's make a lot of money!! Let's make a lot of money!!! Let's make a lot of money, because then I can have all these toys. Let's get money. There's lots of money to be made.*

You have heard people say money does not buy happiness. It is true...it only buys quick fixes for those choosing to live in destructive emotions, thoughts and actions for the sake of money itself.

Those who are happy and have money are happy because of the enjoyment they get attracting it, and they enjoy the emotions, the thoughts and the actions, exchanging more money energy to get more things or do more activities. They are using the Laws of Energy, Vibrations and Attraction constructively. They understand there is an unlimited supply of energy in the universe! They understand the law! They truly love life!

Then there is the mass consciousness of mankind that says, *"Why am I not happy?"* You're not happy because you haven't allowed yourself to love God/Life, yourself and others unconditionally. You haven't been doing what's important to you. When you do what's important to you, guess what happens? You get the money! You get money that really makes you happy. People who are successful have money no matter what people say is happening in the world. No matter what the media says. No matter what the stock market is saying. Successful people always attract money no matter what the so-called "charts and graphs on what's going on in the world with money" say—because they're doing what they love to do.

Life ABSOLUTES

That passion that drives them is there every single day and they're doing what they love. When you're doing what you passionately love, money will come as long as you are not worried about it, as long as you do not have any attachment, as long as you feel worthy to receive it.

NOW, this chapter is about attracting and keeping abundance....not just about money!

Hopefully you have already figured out the answer of how to attract and keep abundance from all the "hints" given in all the other chapters. Did you come directly to this chapter? Then you are going to want to read at least the first eight chapters. I suggest reading all of the previous chapters. They are in the order that they are for a reason!

Attracting abundance is simple. As simple as your ABC's. Live the correct formula of life and you will have abundance. What is that formula? Once again, life energy qualified with positive emotions creates positive thoughts, which create positive spoken words and actions thus creating a positive outcome. Take that formula and read it like this: *I do what I love and I love what I do.* You have heard this before.

TRUTH: Abundance is attracted to you by your life energy's rate of vibration. YOU put your attention on what you want and attract it back to YOU! YOU put your attention on constructive qualities and take the actions required, the abundance floods into your world by the law of energy and vibration plus the law of attraction, thus creating the one Law of Life. Love with all your heart, mind and being the Creator of All Life and thou shalt be provided for! Life gives back to you what you give to life! Reap what you sow.

Abundance is energy that has taken on the physical manifestation of jewels, money, gold, silver, water, earth, food, clothes, cars, trees, flowers, birds, anything you see that is perfection that gives joy and happiness to life is abundance. Anything you feel that gives love, joy and happiness to life is abundance!!! More importantly, that which

Attracting Abundance

you do not see, that which is God, those who are Angels, those who are higher beings are part of the unlimited abundance in the universe.

Do you realize you are already abundant? YOU are! Everything you see that you enjoy is abundance there for you to enjoy. Do you "have to" so called "own it" in order to enjoy it? NO, not always!!! In reality you never really own anything. You cannot take it with you, therefore you do not own it! The only thing you take with you is your life energy, which is the real you.

Now that being said, you want the material abundance of the world? Well, then. Bless everything around you with love, peace and happiness. Bless life. Stop abusing it! The more you misuse life the less you will have. The more you bless it and allow it to serve the greater whole the more you will have. Life (your energy) always returns to you more of what you put out. Yes? Yes. You have learned that lesson loud and clear prior to this chapter. Then, bless your money when you circulate it. Tell it to go out and uplift mankind. Bring joy and happiness to all it reaches and touches. Bless the belongings you have and when you use them. Do not horde your blessings...you will get less. Let their beauty and joy uplift others. Let them serve life too.

Example, people have special dishes for special holidays...well, what happens should one of the plates get broken? The room goes quiet. Gasps go out! Well, had the dishes been enjoyed once a week instead of once a year the joy of the beautiful dishes would have been enjoyed and fully appreciated. Instead, using them becomes a negative energy with fear around them, and the dishes have not been enjoyed as much as they could have been. Thus, the owner never really gets the full value of the dishes.

Is it not the same when someone passes away and a person says, *"If I had only spent more time with that person?"* YOU missed out on that abundance, why? It was your freedom of choice...NO excuses!

TRUTH: Live your life, every moment of it enjoying it! Blessing life. Loving life! Appreciating life! Now, you know the formula. The

Life ABSOLUTES

aforementioned are all done with the knowing, *I reap what I sow.* Positive returns positive.

Abundance, dear friends, is yours! You have always had it! You will always have it should you see through the eyes of love, joy, compassion, purity and forgiveness. Be love in action—all the things you desire will come to you. You are the magnet through your attention. Put your attention on what it is you want that will uplift your life and those of mankind and Take Action. The greater is always lifting up the lesser; it is the law of life. When your desires are pure, the "how" will be revealed to you. When your desires are driven by Divine Love the right opportunities will appear in your life like magic or miracles.

Miracles are the way the laws of life work when you are working with the laws of life. Miracles are the way all life should *outpicture*. Divine Love is that which is called "a miracle." You are created from Divine Love-Life-Energy. Therefore, the natural attraction is that it attracts itself back to you. YOU and only you have been in the way of its return to you and following through you—through your use of negative emotions thus creating the destructive formula of lack and limitation in your world.

That being said, it does not matter what appears to be in your world. Focus your attention on your desires and keep it there and know that through your attention on the giver of all life, your love returned to the giver, your gratitude returned to the giver. The giver will then be the doer through you and for you! The giver is the knower of all that is and will tell you the *how's*, the *why's*, and the *when's*—action will be easy. That is you being in the flow, when you finally realize that you must allow life to work through you unobstructed by your negative emotions!

Since abundance is Life's (God's) wealth to the world, it is unlimited from the side of the invisible! It is unlimited!!! Ever expanding. It is your responsibility to expand it through constructive use. You expand it through constructive use by using it to glorify God, and by doing well for mankind.

Attracting Abundance

Do not worry yourself over the appearance of the outer world. There is no lack on the side of God/Life. YOU were promised paradise. It is up to you to demand it, expect it, accept it, and be grateful for it and appreciate. Then the abundance in your world will be greater than all the water in the oceans put together.

Note: Abundance is not just money. Some people are so incredibly abundant and are not millionaires and they are happy beyond their wildest dreams. Get over the human concept that money is the only abundance! Money is energy. We exchange energy/money for other energy. It's ALL energy vibrating at different rates...that is what gives it different appearances. Seriously contemplate this TRUTH and you will rejoice in how abundant you are and you will easily increase your abundance every day with little to no effort.

When you attract money, it stays as long as you love it just for the sake of being loved, appreciated. Do not confuse attachment as love. When you have an attachment to it, you actually start repelling it! Attachment equals fear of lack—fear of losing it! The "human" thinks somehow it cannot live without it or be happy without it. **The only thing you cannot live without is God. And that is impossible because we are made up of God's life and can NEVER become separate from it no matter how hard the human attempts to sabotage.** We are all one with creation and always will be, therefore, why not embrace it? Thank it. Love it and let it flow unobstructed and abundantly into our lives and out into all life for the upliftment of all mankind, thus creating heaven manifests once again EVERYWHERE here on earth to stay permanently!

OK...you still want to know more about money attraction. When you're chasing money out of a feeling of, *"I don't have enough money,"* or out of greed, you might get the quick fix, then you wake up one day and you have less. You have less. Lots of people lost lots of money in the last couple years because it was a quick fix. Example: huge stock market earnings and lottery winnings. The people, who used their money wisely, still have money.

Life ABSOLUTES

So when you have what you perceive to be lack, people say, *"Oh my goodness I am so broke. I don't have any money."* What are you focusing on? The negative. You're focusing on what you don't desire, and you're only going to create more of that because when you're declaring to the world, *"I don't have money,"* what are you doing? You're putting out energy that says, *"Push all the money away from me, because I'm saying I don't have any, so don't bring me any more money!"*

That negative energy goes out and says, *"I'm going to attract less money."* So what happens is when you desire to attract more money, be grateful for the money that you have. I'm so very grateful for this five-dollar bill I have in my wallet. I am so grateful for it. When you're grateful for that, you're being positive about money. You get more money then. I'm the one who picks up the pennies on the street, because I honor money. I'm grateful that penny's there. You know what? You're too good to pick up that penny, then the universe says, *"Guess what? Then you don't get the hundred dollars, the thousand dollars, the hundred thousand dollars, because you think you're better than a penny? I'll show you what you're worth."* So, I pick up the pennies. I pick up the dimes. I pick up the quarters. When I go out on walks I say, *"Wow, I made thirty-six cents today walking. This is cool! I got paid to walk! I love it!"*

So it's finding gratitude for what you have. Be grateful for the money that you have. Be grateful for what you're getting. You'll then get more.

Another way that people push money out of their lives is to assume that other people don't have money. When you assume people don't have money, then they're going to present themselves to you in that nature. You assume someone doesn't have money—I've seen some of the wealthiest people in the world, you know, dressed like somebody who probably has five cents to their name. So when you assume that people don't have money, they're not going to desire to share their money with you. And we live in a world where we exchange money. So first of all, start accepting the TRUTH that you have money.   Be grateful for the money you have.   And then

Attracting Abundance

acknowledge that everybody else in the world has money also. We all have money. And be grateful that everybody else has money.

And then, here's another stickler that really gets in the way of your money flow. When you pay your bills? How many people are happy when they pay their bills? *It feels good when I pay my bills!*

Good! When you pay that electricity bill, you should be grateful that you have something to put electricity into, whether it's an apartment, whether it's a house. And you know what else you're doing when you pay that electricity bill? You're employing people. You didn't know that you were an employer, did you? You're employing the people at the electric company. You're employing the people at the water company. You're employing the people at the garbage company. Every single time you write a check during the month to pay your bills, you're employing people. You're circulating energy.

"Karen, I have been grateful when paying my monthly bills and now to my surprise, yet not a surprise from what you told us at our company seminar. I have MORE money NOW!" –Jennifer C.

You want to be happy and grateful that you're paying that bill, that you get that opportunity to do that. You get to share that money. And because you are hoping people are going to share their money back, they're going to come in and buy items. That's a form of sharing money. You're happily sharing your money—you go out and you buy a coat, you buy a dinner, and you're happy to share that money. The world works on circulation. You flow money, you'll get money back.

When you're tight with your money, or being greedy, you're cutting off your energy supply that could attract supply back to you. Instead of letting it flow out through generosity and receiving more in return you get a little trickle back.

When you feel good about sharing your money—and I'm not talking about the quick fix of going out and spending money that in reality you know you shouldn't be spending—you're circulating money

Life ABSOLUTES

in a constructive manner, a positive manner, it's just flowing, and it comes back to you. It comes back to you. In one way, shape or form, it comes back to you as abundance. Note: *Spend* is a lack word. *Circulate* is a word of abundance because you are giving to another part of life.

So when you desire to be positive about your money, that money can flow into your bank account, it can flow into your hands, and you can have that money because it's still there. It didn't go anywhere. It's always been there. It shifts. It flows. And it goes to those people who are constructive and positive and grateful for it. That's where that money goes. Those people who get money out of greed don't keep it for very long. They don't keep the money for very long. It's the quick fix. It's the quick fix!

So it's about perception. And I bring up the money issue, because that seems to be the biggest thing that we all desire money in our world, because money is an exchange that we use. The barter system is back in fashion nowadays, but money still is the international way of doing business, so we always desire to say, *"Well, how do I get more money in my life?"* That's how you get it.

It's freedom.

Absolutely. It's freedom. Absolutely. And freedom comes from freedom of choice. That's what I've been talking to you about. You have the freedom to choose what you're going to put your attention on. Either put your attention on the TRUTH that you always have money, and you always will have money, you've always been able to attract money, and you're going to continue to be able to make money, or, have a pity party and say *"I'm so broke, I'm so poor, I can't believe it, I can't afford anything, life is unfair."* Then that's what you will continue to get. And the reason that you end up with lack in your life is you do not live in the state of Divine Love in action. No excuses. Excuses are created by the EGO.

Once again, I share with you. YOU as a creator with God have not only the ability to create and attract abundance, it is your duty in

Attracting Abundance

life to expand it! That is the reason you are here, to expand the perfection of life, to expand the existence of Divine Love. Your body is a channel, a vehicle, a vessel through which life expands and creates greater perfection for the rest of life! When you answer the call that has been calling from within since birth, you will be free from all human creation of lack and limitation and will truly live in heaven for all eternity.

Why not start today?! It is your birthright! What are you waiting for? Being born was your invitation! Start living your life of joy, happiness, abundance and better health! Live it! Breathe it! Visualize it! Expect it! Accept it! Experience it! Enjoy your relationships, enjoy your career, enjoy your health, enjoy your wealth and most of all enjoy your relationship with God. **BE LOVE IN ACTION RIGHT NOW!!!**

TRUTHS RECAP: $[(e^E) T]A = Outcome$

- I am a magnet that attracts what I put out.
- I give all credit to the life-God for the abundance in my life.
- I am grateful for all the abundance I have used, have and will have!
- I bless all life, especially my abundance!
- I am the outpicturing of my emotionally driven thoughts and actions.
- The only thing I cannot live without is God. And that is impossible because I am made up of God's life and can NEVER become separate from it no matter how vehemently the human sabotages.
- _____
  _____
  _____
- _____
  _____
  _____
  _____

Life ABSOLUTES

"Yes! I enjoyed your book, 'Life ABSOLUTES' very much and will read again and again. Karen- Today was Absolutely wonderful. When I am doing my work I am in total bliss-heaven.

Also, I love the audio book. It allows me to stay on track guiding me in a way that assists me in staying out of the negative, judgment and the human traps that can sabotage my life. What I love is some days I may feel out of sorts not really clear as to exactly what it is that is causing my 'imbalance'-I just allow my inner voice to guide me to the CD that is right for that day and it is always the one that helps me to get back to where I need to be—guiding me and allowing me to find what I need to adjust in myself.

I could not listen to this audio book enough. Every time I gleam something new that assists me in being one with my source and inline with the path I am meant to follow. Thank you! Thank you! Thank you!" -Cheri Atkinson

CHAPTER 19

BEING FEARLESS

THE SILENT POWER

Being Fearless is a silent power. One does not walk around stating, *"I am fearless."* —it just emits out of the person.

I chose this topic because it has become very clear to me that so many people are perfecting skills, gaining mastery in many avenues to gain success in their lives, and yet such a small percentage of the population is successful, truly successful. Yet, so many are skilled! So many are proficient at what they have trained to be able to do. So many have the ability to execute the fundamentals of their craft, their heart's desire and yet still are not succeeding! Why? You guessed it—FEAR.

Fear—too funny that the human seems to have this desire to be scared on purpose according to all the so-called popular TV shows and movies being made that are horror/thriller based. And yet, it is just that—FEAR—that is sabotaging the masses. Irony? Perhaps the human thinks if it can be fearless when it comes to "pretend" fears of the movie industry and grotesques displays of human behavior by eating, touching and experiencing acts of degradation in public for money, that the real fears that lurk inside their very being will disappear for the moment or seem a little less real? Think about it.

Are we indeed inviting the fear element to take hold of us as a society even more by watching all these reality TV shows, crime shows, violent shows, war news—all centered around VIOLENCE and violent behavior? Is that not what terrorism is about? Are we not as a society terrorizing ourselves on purpose every day for a quick fix of adrenaline? Are we not saying to the terror-fear beast—*"Bring it on!? We like to be scared! We like to feel helpless!"* Why?

Why, are we tearing down the very fiber of our being for the sake of

Life ABSOLUTES

a quick fix? Why? Because then you, me, our society do not face the real fear! The fear of failure, the fear of success. The fear that one has picked the wrong career. The fear that one might be wrong. The fear that ....you fill in the blank.

I say, STOP the insanity! STOP watching violence for fun. You are attracting fear into your world, OUR world. Face your fears. What is fear? FEAR is a perception inside the human intellect of the one having the fear. Fear is the mass consciousness buying into false propaganda. FEAR is the EGO lying. Fear is the belief another human has control over your destiny! That is a lie. YOU are the authority of your world. Take CHARGE!

So, STOP—once and for all—giving power to other's opinions and better yet, stop the VOICE that runs around in your head sabotaging you. They are lies. Isn't that the biggest complaint we hear people talking about right now—how this person lied and that person lied? Then why is it OK for you to lie to yourself? Are you not being a hypocrite?

Being fearless begins with listening to the truth within your heart—the truth of love-Divine Love. Therein always lies the truth. There in the silence of Divine Love is the wisdom and power to overcome any human obstacle. There YOU can overcome the human fear of doubt. There the truth becomes very clear that there is no lack in your world. There lies the truth that there is NO limitation to what you can achieve. For oneness with God is fearlessness. Oneness with God is the letting go. Oneness with God is the trust that all things are good. Oneness with God is perfection in your world no matter what the rest of the world is doing. Oneness with God is the knowing, *"I am in this world but not of it."* Be in the silence of God's voice and therein lies the power of fearlessness, for within love nothing else can exist that is not perfection, and fear, doubt, worthlessness, lack and limitation are not created from love, they are created from lack of love—FEAR.

I implore you to stop inviting the fear element into your lives! Stop buying into the lies of other's fears, lack, doubt and limitations.

Being Fearless

STOP believing the destructive thoughts you verbalize inside your head when you think no one else can hear. God/Life can hear it! STOP ALL THE LIES and become fearless. Anything that is felt or expressed that is less than perfection of Divine Love is a lie. And it comes from fear-selfishness. Stop the fear and hate within yourself. Encourage your fellow man to do the same and the terror will stop. Stop sabotaging the love of God from flowing into you and working through you. Stand tall and humble and be a servant of God. Speak only the truth. Speak only words of kindness, compassion, hope and love and then you will be fearless and all will know.

Then your skills, your proficiency of your trade, your career, your relationships, your passions will shine forth with confidence and return to you the abundance of success you could barely imagine. The truth of true success lies in the truth of the heart which must come forth and be shared with all of mankind. **We are here to uplift the whole!**

What, you don't believe me? Be one with God for 40 days and prove me wrong. You do believe. Incoming miracles for YOU!

TRUTHS RECAP: $[(e^E)\ T]A = Outcome$

- I say, STOP the insanity! STOP watching violence for fun. I face my fears. FEAR is ONLY a perception inside my intellect. Fear is the mass consciousness buying into false propaganda. FEAR is the EGO lying. Fear is the belief another human has control over my destiny! That is a lie. I am the authority of my world through love.
- Being fearless begins with listening to the truth within my heart—the truth of love-Divine Love. Therein always lies the truth.
- I will no longer lie to myself.
- _____
  _____
- _____
  _____
  _____

Life ABSOLUTES

- _____
  _____
  _____
  _____

CHAPTER 20

NO SUCH THING AS A SECRET

ENERGY HEARS

Can you keep a secret? How many times has some one asked you that question? Well, dear ones there is no such thing as a secret.

Let's get very clear about this—there is NO such thing as a secret! Life is made up of energy and energy is what makes up the world you live in. So even the deepest so called secrets you feel and think in the private places of your being are not a secret from life!

Why am I sharing this with you? Because some people think it is OK to feel and think about that which is destructive in their emotions and thoughts as long as they do not act on them or speak them. FALSE.

TRUTH: Energy is energy. You use it to feel, you use it to think and therefore it has been qualified with that quality and does go forth and create in your world. As you sow, so shall you reap. Even that which is created in the silence comes forth for the whole world to witness. Life returns to its qualifier that which it was qualified with.

So, I offer out to you. Be aware of the random emotions and thoughts sabotaging your life, your relationships, career, finances and health. Be aware that they are just as powerful, perhaps more powerful at times than the feelings and spoken words acted upon, because the feelings kept inside can gather a powerful momentum of energy!

How many times a day do you lie to yourself, *I am stupid, I am fat, I am poor, I am broke, I am angry, I am*...? How many times do you say something destructive about another person? Be honest...it is about time for the elections again...are you saying judgmental things, feeling hate, anger, contempt? Sure it is human. Therein lies the problem and the solution. The human is not perfect and the whole divine plan is to return back to the perfection from whence we

Life ABSOLUTES

came.

Stop using that excuse, *"I can't be perfect"* —it is just that—an excuse! Remember, you reap what you sow.

So, sow in silence, words of love, compassion, mercy and forgiveness. How about tossing in some praise and gratitude too! Offer up feelings and thoughts that the country leaders, bosses, your spouse, friends, family members, strangers and your so-called enemies find divine love in their hearts and live by that law. Bless them instead of judging them. Be in the NOW. Remember all life is one.

Being in the NOW is being one with God. Then the chatter that is destructive is silenced and Silence is Golden! Did you know the color gold is the color of peace? So Silence is Peace. Since there are no secrets, your destructive unspoken emotions and thoughts still reach the person, place or thing that you are putting your attention on, thus you are transmitting your negative energy! YOU are still accountable for the destruction of another life when that is what you are doing in the silence.

Image 49

No Such Thing As A Secret

Now, before you let your EGO get all up in arms, remember that it is your choice to create what you will in your world, and you will live with for the rest of your life. Is it worth it to destroy yourself for the sake of your EGO? Is it worth it to sabotage yourself, your dreams, your relationships and your country for the sake of the EGO? After all it is your choice. I hope you choose the causeless cause of love. So, when you think you have a "secret, let it be one that makes you smile and know that you want to share it with the world—for the so-called secret will be *"I love Life and Life loves me.!"* Oh, what a wonderful world!

What are your so-called secrets? Let them go. Fix them and move on to NO more "secrets" that destroy you, our Nation and mankind. At all times, love yourself, your neighbor and your so-called enemy—then you will truly love your father. You will be blessed with more than you will ever require!

TRUTHS RECAP: $[(e^E)\ T]A=Outcome$

- There is no such thing as a secret.
- Even my emotions and thoughts experienced in silence, "in secret," create in my world!
- At all times, I will love myself, my neighbor and my so-called enemy—then I will truly love my Divine Creator. I will be blessed with more than I will ever require!
- _____
- _____
- _____

Life ABSOLUTES

What secrets are you supposedly keeping? Write them down and then eradicate the ones that are negative.

My Wake Up Call

CHAPTER 21

MY WAKE UP CALL

ASKING FOR HELP

Client: Do you want to share with us what that wake-up call was?

(Remember that I am sharing this in third person so as not to bring the negative energy back into my world again. This is the Karen that was, not the Karen that is)

Absolutely. As I shared earlier with you, one of the last things that happened to Karen in her negative spiral was a car accident that took her health from her, and in hindsight it was perhaps a small thing, but she is a person that's very physical, very high energy, likes to go, likes to be able to be active, and Karen shattered her shoulder and tore her rotator cuff, which probably seems kind of small. It wasn't like Karen injured her spine or anything—however it made her incapacitated. The doctors put her on lots of pain killers and drugs, and she eventually took herself off of them. The left side of her body was numb, and Karen had migraine headaches every day for a couple of years.

Karen got very angry about that accident instead of realizing that it was a wake-up call in her life, Karen had the pity party. Karen was angry at the lawyer, angry at the doctors for lying and saying she wasn't hurt. Karen was angry, and so the angrier she got, the more negative things started happening around her situation, until one day she hit rock bottom. One day Karen was sitting in her house, and she decided she didn't want to be on the planet anymore. Note, the car accident did not start the negative spiral…it was just the last rung of the ladder before she hit rock bottom. Karen had known five or six people who had committed suicide and she had decided that wasn't an option for her. But Karen did not want to be on this planet. She didn't want to be here because she wasn't a productive person. Karen was very miserable—depressed—numb. She just didn't have a single

Life ABSOLUTES

thing to be grateful for in her life, or so she thought.

And that was the darkest and the brightest moment, because Karen literally screamed out at God—she was very angry, and she wanted answers, and she wanted them now. Karen demanded to be taken from the earth or be given answers. She was in the most emotional pain she had EVER experienced!

Guess what? Karen got answers, and she got them fast and furious. And the first thing that she did was love God and start being grateful—because she had felt God's love for the first time in a long time. Really, felt it! So the first step out of the darkness was loving God and then being grateful. The crying out was the letting go of the human EGO. This was the final letting go of the EGO, saying God is greater than anything mankind can give or offer me. Karen is nothing without God!

At first she sat there on the steps of her house searching for anything to be grateful for. Karen was so far down the pity party ladder that the EGO had led her to believe that she had nothing. That was a HUGE party she had been having for herself.

Finally, Karen came up with one thing to be grateful for and it was like a ray of light shining through—that was God's love. Then she was able to feel more gratitude. She obviously, was grateful for her family because they were the reason she would not take her own life. You see Karen had shut them out because she did not want them to see her so pitiful…well, that is EGO. That was pride—shame. That was fear! Believe me her family helped her a lot and so did her friends. Karen was the one that pulled away! Not them.

However, Karen did finally ask for help from GOD, through gratitude (gratitude is a form of love). She started to love God more and love herself again. And Karen had pushed that all by the wayside because of her pity party. Karen had thrown it all away. Karen didn't answer the phone anymore. Karen didn't do anything, because Karen was just in so much pain and it was all about that in her world and Karen forgot to focus on what she had. She focused on her injury and

My Wake Up Call

all about "woe is me". She pretty much self-destructed because she didn't want to live anymore. Granted this pity party was the icing on the cake to all the negative energy Karen had attracted over the years through all her negative choices. Karen's boat had sunk! Karen started to drown and almost gave up...almost is the key word. Never give up!!!

So I started learning how to be grateful. When I started learning how to be grateful, I started pulling myself out and pulling myself up, and that's when I decided to start teaching this message to people so that they wouldn't self-destruct like I almost had. I realized I always had two choices—positive or negative. My God voice, the Presence within me reminded me of the formula every day and it still does ☺

TRUTH: My mission in life is to be the person who goes out and uplifts other people. To go out and give people positive, constructive ways to change their lives; to fulfill that passion and desire that you have in life; to be the person who loves who you are; to really love who you are; to really be excited about what it is that you do in your life. To recognize there is that which is more powerful than you and gives you life and everything that is good. And that life does not judge or punish. It reacts to you—your choices—your accountability. You came from that source of perfection and it is your life purpose to return to that perfection. Arise out of the lack and limitation that you and mankind have created and rise up into the perfection from whence you came. Remember, the life force that flows through you is perfect—allow it to stay perfect and flow through you and out to all mankind and everything in existence.

I am on that journey and believe me it is so much better than going the other direction, which was at one time Karen's living hell. Awaken, arise and enjoy the blessings life has to give you. With fierce determination, in every moment of every day choose LOVE. You will have nothing to regret and everything to gain—blessings will abound in your life and your cup will runneth over!

Note: At one time in my life I was very happy. However, it was the silent killers that Karen allowed in that almost took her physical

Life ABSOLUTES

being away. Ever since I can remember I just wanted to be happy, and I wanted other people to be happy, but Karen was tricked by the lies of our society and the EGO. Be on guard. Be aware of your emotions. Be aware of where you are putting your attention/energy and make sure it is positive—long-term positive!

Should you require help outside of this book please get it! Please ask for help! Every life is Priceless and people do care—I care, you matter to mankind!

Suicide Prevention: 1-800-SUICIDE

> *"When there is nothing left but God that is when you find out that God is all you require."* -Unknown

Image 50...do you know what it is?

CHAPTER 22

IN CLOSING

A COUPLE OF STORIES

Visualize that you have a balloon. You're in your life, and you're doing all these positive wonderful things—your balloon starts filling up with air. You know that goal list that you have? Well in your life, you're doing all these positive things, and when you do a positive thing your balloon is closer to where it's supposed to be. We do another positive thing: *"Oh, we're almost there. This is so exciting!"*

And then all of a sudden, we're telling somebody how exciting it is. *"Oh I'm so close to my goal! This is so great!"* And that person comes along and they start saying, *"Oh my goodness what happens when you get there? You're not going to be able to stay there."* And you start getting this fear and this doubt and you start worrying and you start judging.

(Pop!)

Just like that, it went away. You destroyed it. You let the air out of your dream. You destroyed your dream just like that: by buying into fear, doubt, anger, selfishness, and jealousy, you destroyed what you were doing. The nice thing is the second you get back on track, you have a fresh new balloon, and it gets inflated again, and you still get to reach that goal, because you have that choice. When most people pop their balloon, that's when they sit down and have a pity party.

I'm here to tell you that when you get on that momentum of going in the direction you're going, it's easier to stay there. Remember I said earlier that a rocket uses over 90% of its fuel on blast-off. The other 10% is used to do the whole orbit and return. As individuals, the greatest amount of your energy that you use is starting.—starting that goal that you set for yourself. Once you start you're in that place of momentum because that positive energy is coming back to you,

Life ABSOLUTES

and that helps you be a better person. And when you start setting those goals and start achieving them, you know what happens? You become this big walking magnet of positive energy! People start coming into your life to help you. They come into your life and say, *"Know what?, I have a contact for you. I have some information for you. I have a program that you might be interested in. You can be actually applying the skills that you're learning while you're going to school."* People come into your life and start helping you. That's why successful people hang out with successful people.

It's not because they're snobs. Karen used to think they were snobs at one point in her life because Karen was jealous. In reality, successful people hang out with other successful people because it's like a magnet. Success draws success. Positive draws positive.

So I'm here to tell you, you can have anything you desire in your world. It's your choice. You make the choice, right here, right now. In every moment of every day, and ask yourself, *"Am I living from the motivation of love? Is love the power, the emotion that is driving my actions and my thoughts?"*

So that is what this saying means: *I am the outpicturing of my emotionally driven thoughts and actions.* When I am in a state of love, I'm outpicturing loving things in my world. When you are angry and defensive, you're outpicturing disasters in your world. So, you get to choose what you're going to outpicture, right here, right now, and the best thing to do is have compassion for other people.

This story was shared with me. A woman was going through the grocery line. She's at the check-out, and the person in front of her is

In Closing

purchasing her groceries, and the teller is really rude, making mistakes and the customer has to correct her and then she is defensive about it. The customer ahead of her ends up leaving with her groceries. Now she, the customer, gets up to pay for her groceries and the same experience happens. The checker's just rude and she's kind of defensive and she's not happy. The lady pays for her groceries and she's walking out with the box boy and she turns to the box boy and she says, *"Oh my goodness why would anybody employ somebody like that? That's terrible for the business! I can't believe that!"*

And the box boy turns to her and says, *"You know, her little boy got hit by a car on his bicycle before she came to work today. He's in the emergency room. She has to be here because she doesn't have the money to cover the deductible on her health insurance."*

So we don't know what's going on in somebody else's life. When we see this perception that somebody's doing this horrible, horrendous thing, and their behavior isn't the way that you perceive it should be, we judge. Next time you find yourself judging, stop a moment and have compassion. Maybe you can be a more helpful to that person when you choose compassion. Maybe they don't have enough knowledge. Maybe they're requiring some assistance. Maybe all they could use right at that time is a big hug and a smile or perhaps a silent prayer.

"Keep your face in the sunshine and you can never see the shadow."
-Helen Keller

Another story, a smile is worth a bazillion dollars—more than that, a smile is priceless!!! When Karen was in school, Karen was extremely shy and the biggest thing that she was so excited about, when she'd get home from school was that she had smiled and said "hi" to people at school. It was a huge accomplishment for her.

A couple of years back, my mom told me that a person whom I went to school with came up and told her, that because I (the shy Karen) had smiled and said hello to her, it kept her from committing suicide.

Life ABSOLUTES

I know in my heart that favor was returned to me in my moment of darkness—it came back to me. **A simple smile from God.** A smile doesn't cost you anything. It's effortless and it can save so many people's lives. It can make so many people's day **<u>brighter!</u>**

Remember, everyone is doing the best that they can do. Yes, they are. We all believe at each moment in time we are doing our best…hindsight tells us differently at times. In the moment we are doing our best with the knowledge we have, with the strength we have and with the love that we feel. So smile as much as you can, at as many people as you can. Save a life today! Live in a place of compassion, forgiveness, praise and love and when you're constantly being love in action, your world will be successful, your careers will be successful, your relationships will be successful, your health is going to be successful and your abundance will be successful.

So I offer to you today to love God, love yourself and love others and remember being a pure loving person is FUN!!! It really is. When you hit that bump in the road and it's like, *"Oh my goodness. Hummmm, I can be miserable or I can be having fun. What do I desire?"* Choose the quickest and most positive way to get back to the state of having fun-love in action! There are only two choices in life: Constructive or destructive—choose constructive and YOU are then a Master. You are then allowing perfection to be and you are walking the path. Keep calling upon the greater perfection of life to be in charge— "be" in, through, and around you at all times. Keep your attention on that which is perfection and your calls will be answered. Be in service to God: Love, light and life and be grateful.

May the Love and Light of Life-God flood in, through and around you and raise you out of your discord, lack and limitation and into the light of eternal happiness—heaven made manifest here on earth! Angels walk with you!

In service to the Most High, the source of all Life—

In Closing

CHAPTER 23

Q & A

LIVE CONVERSATIONS

How can I make people (like the person I love) understand these laws?

Karen: When you're in a relationship with another person, you're like, *"Well I love them: They don't love me back."* You don't get to control what other people do. You only get to control your world. You can control what you put out. That person may not desire to love you back; they have that freedom of choice. They get to decide. When you are being a loving, giving, compassionate person, the probability of people in your world being that way back to you is very high. OK? There are going to be some of those people who come back and just desire to be negative, and that's their choice. This is not about going out now and converting the world by forcing it down somebody's throat, because you can't force it down somebody's throat. We can teach by our own actions and be uplifting. We can give people information and the ultimate end result is they get to make the choice. They have to make the choice of how they desire to live in their world. So in relationships, you can't force somebody to change. When you desire to lose weight, the only way you can lose it is because you made the choice. You desire to make money. The only way you can make money is because you made the choice.

So it's about the choices that you're making. We cannot control other people. And when you're attempting to control other people, you're taking their freedom away, so what happens in return? You have less freedom because it comes back to you. Say you desire to go out and start controlling people, what happens? They attempt to control you. So it becomes a control issue problem. And then nobody's happy.

Life ABSOLUTES

Charity work... There are a lot of people who go out and they say, *"I'm going to do charity work so I can feel better about myself. I don't feel any better!"* Well, because they did it expecting something in return. When you give because you expect something in return, you don't get it. When you give freely, then you get back. Because when you give expecting something in return, it's coming from a negative place. You're coming from a place of lack. When you're in a place of lack you get more lack. *"I love that person, and I feel empty."* Why do you feel empty? Because you don't love yourself. You must love yourself before you can feel that love back.

So how do you love yourself? You start praising yourself. This is not about ego when you praise yourself for the qualities that you like about yourself. Praise is very healthy. We want to acknowledge within ourselves these are all the wonderful things about me. These are all the wonderful skills that I have. Then you can point out the things to yourself, maybe the things you desire to change. You're happy that you know that you desire to change those things, because when you acknowledge things that you desire to change, it's a very positive thing. You can move those over into the constructive side of your personality. We all have things that come into our awareness at some point in our life that we should probably change about ourselves, and that's a positive thing.

GUEST: *I just want to go back to what you said about whenever you give anything, you shouldn't expect anything in return. Just to clarify that in my mind, so, I mean—give freely.*

Karen: There's an obvious exchange I gave $12 for this particular item, I should be getting that item back.

GUEST*: So then where does that stop and start? Or does it?*

Karen: In relationships, say I'm giving love to a person? I'm not guaranteed to get that back. You go out and do charity work it doesn't mean that everybody in the room is going to come up and hug you and say thank you. You did it just because you desired to give. I'm talking about personal relationships. You're talking about

In Closing

giving something monetary (money) for a product or service, then, yes, that was the agreement, I gave $12, and I'm supposed to get that box back, yes. I'm talking about emotional return.

GUEST: *So I should have no expectations going into a personal relationship, interaction, or whatever, just out of curiosity, is that what you're saying?*

Karen: Absolutely. **You cannot change that person.** A lot of people say, *"I really love that person. When I get married, then I can change them."*

GUEST 2: *I can give you a perfect example. At my horse barn —our horse trainer, who doesn't have a lot of money, was in a car accident—whiplash—two weeks ago. And I don't have to do this, but I chose to clean her stalls and feed her horses every night after work. And I volunteered to do this openly and free heartedly, not expecting anything back. I don't expect free riding lessons. I don't expect money. I don't expect anything back, because I'm doing this truly from the heart and it's something that I desire to do to help her.*

GUEST: *Doesn't it make you feel good?*

GUEST 2: *Oh yeah. Every single day I feel good knowing that I have done that.*

GUEST: *That's awesome. I just thought I understood her saying that you shouldn't expect to feel good.*

Karen: Oh, OK! I understand the question. You'll feel good. You'll feel good and that's OK. That's OK. It's about how you feel; it's not about whether somebody reciprocates.

Automatically, you get something back, because the energy flows. You don't get to control where or when it returns to you. So, you automatically **get joy out of giving.** You automatically get satisfaction out of giving when you give from a place of love. You automatically get that. **That's the reward.** Say somebody's

Life ABSOLUTES

physically going to come up and say, *"Thank you,"* or somebody's going to give you something in return, for giving freely, that's not a guarantee. So you give and do charity, or you uplift people because you just desire to. You can't demand. People say, *"Well I did this for you three months ago!"*

They're keeping score. You give because you desire to give, and the return on that is you feel good about that giving. That's the return. OK? I'm glad you asked for that clarification.

So praise yourself for the things that you do well. Then you want to praise others. Praise others. Start focusing on the wonderful things that other people do. Focus on the positive things that other people do, because when somebody tells me I did something well, gosh that makes me feel good, and then I desire to do more of that. So when you praise people for what they're doing well, it enables them to do more of that. And what happens is when we're getting praise, then we're more open to those instructional things, you know, let's have some growth in this area. Let's have some growth in this area. Then we're open to getting better at what we do as individuals. Say somebody was to say to you, *"Gosh, you're really good at doing this and let's work on getting better at that."* When you are used to getting praise all the time, you're open to constructive suggestions from others.

What happens is, when you're constantly being told, *"You're not doing this right,"* *"You're not doing this right,"* *"You're not doing this right,"* *"You're not doing this right,"* you get defensive. And so you don't desire to grow—and you don't hear what somebody might have to say that's constructive, that would really; really help you, because you became a defensive person.

So have a nice balance in your life. Give more on the praise side than on the "You want to fix this. You want to be better at that." We become healthier people when we are surrounded by praise and give praise. Then we're open to opportunities and information to be better at something else that we're doing —to be better at something else that we're doing, because in our relationships, career, and health...

In Closing

there's always going to be a time that we want to be better at them. That's what growth is about. We are here to expand our perfection.

In relationships, say you praise what you like about the other person on a regular basis. Then in the future perhaps when there's something that you'd like changed, perhaps that person will be more open to change, because they're not on the defensive. When they do not hear praise, what happens is eventually, the layers of that onion I was talking about become really, really thick and they're always on the defensive. And I'm here to tell you. You're in an environment where people aren't giving you praise, when you are giving <u>yourself</u> praise, it keeps you out of the "defense" mode.

The above kinds of conversations occur when you attend my seminars.

Please checkout my special programs for business, organizations and special events.

Please note there is more knowledge and wisdom with which I have been blessed. I offer it to you and others through private coaching, workshops, video calls, tele-seminars. This book is the foundation of mastery. It is simple and precise. Some people want more answers, more details, higher knowing and more assistance. Ask me to coach and mentor you.

What would you like?   Write down your individualized requirements!

Start writing.

Life ABSOLUTES

Now ask ME!
503.312.0913
lavoie@masteringyourworld.com

CHAPTER 24

MASTERING YOUR WORLD PROGRAM

WORKSHOPS

Workshops are offered as private consults or for groups. All workshops/consults are custom made to the client keeping the fundamental program in place and the client gets to add as many bells and whistles as they want. You want the seminar at the beach, in the mountains, at a Resort, your business, on your private plane, you want it 4 hours, 1 day or a week, you want it for the whole company, the whole team, the whole school or just one person…I do my best to accommodate!

For pricing please call: (503) 312-0913
Or visit my website: www.masteringyourworld.com

SPECIAL OFFERS FOR YOU THE READER

Want to purchase a large quantity of this book—RECEIVE A DISCOUNT. Holding a fundraiser? Call my office: 503-312-0913

CD'S AND MORE

Yes, this book is offered as audio book on CD.

I also offer phone consulting by the hour, week, monthly or special program pricing.

You want me as a guest speaker—ASK! I will do my best to accommodate YOU.

It is my eternal joy to service life and share the blessings of life's knowledge with all that seek it. –Karen LaVoie

Life ABSOLUTES

NEWSLETTER

Sign up for my free inspirational eNewsletter – *"Be The Truth"* at my website: www.masteringyourworld.com

NEXT BOOK AND PRODUCTS

My next book, "Seeds of Light" will be out by 2009.

Please check out my website for valuable tools to assist you on your Exciting new journey!
www.masteringyourworld.com/products.htm

CHAPTER 25
RESOURCE GUIDE AND REFERENCES

Unveiled Mysteries………………..……..Godfre Ray King
The Magic Presence ……………………. Godfre Ray King
The "I AM" Discourses ……... Ascended Master St. Germain

Note: I read these books long after creating the formula for my program. Clients keep asking me, did you read this book and that book. So the quest began for books that would touch upon or offer greater assistance to others or myself. You will be drawn to that which you FEEL/KNOW is the material for you.

The bottom line is you are on a quest for the truth. Sometimes it is right in front of you and you are thrilled you have found it, other times you are passed the place of the information given forth in a particular book on your quest and perhaps you are not ready for the information put before because you have not journeyed far enough. And other times you know what you are reading is not the truth.

Follow your heart. Not your intellect when seeking books to read. Your EGO will at times keep you from the truth. Keep living the truth everyday and the light will become brighter and the truth will appear in the most unexpected ways! I wish you a safe, joyous and speedy journey home!

I have read or listened to materials by the following authors.

Richard Anderson, N.D., N.M.D.
The Bible
Deepak Chopra
Robert Collier
Wayne Dyer
Ester Hicks
Cynthia Kersey
Thomas Moore

Life ABSOLUTES

Suze Orman
Joel Osteen
James Redfield
Spiritual Cinema on-line

About The Author

CHAPTER 26

ABOUT THE AUTHOR

Hello! I've been in the entertainment business for quite a while, and it's my responsibility to be able to get people to understand who they are as an individual. And it was MY first responsibility to understand who I was as an individual and what made me tick. Since acting is about being able to get inside of the "you" through that journey, I started realizing that there's a greater message about acting, and that's learning who you are as a person. And it became very, very apparent to me through this journey and the steps that I went through in my life on how the laws of life work. In conjunction with the awakening I had in my life, I realized we can work with the Universal Laws or against them. And when we're working against them, that's the old "hitting our head against the wall." It takes a lot of energy and causes a lot of pain in our life. And so I decided to take that knowledge that I gained through my journey of being an actress which was actually preparing me to be a speaker. Believe it or not Karen LaVoie used to be extremely shy.

I speak from first-hand experience. At one point, a very low point in Karen's life she sat on the steps of her house in the dark, crying, VERY depressed, and lonely—with no reason to live. She demanded that God take her off the planet. Karen was yelling at God. Karen told God she would not take her own life because Karen knew what pain it would cause her family and friends. Karen demanded that God take her off the planet or give her answers RIGHT NOW! (I talk in third person here for a reason, which was explained in this book.)

I got the answers right then and there and have been applying them and sharing them ever since. I hope this book keeps any and all of you from the human discord experience.

Yes, it is All Good. I do however know I would still be sharing this truth with you, without having had to take that journey! YOU can travel the road that is paved with Divine Love and "Be God/Love in

Life ABSOLUTES

Action in every minute of every day" and live a blessed life, or you can travel the road paved with fear and doubt and eventually awaken to the truth, and get back on the road of Divine Love and live the blessed life or exist in lack and limitation until you leave the physical body. The choice is YOURS. May the information in this book put you or keep you on the path of Divine Love for all eternity. God bless you.

My resume: I have worked with companies and corporations; with a lot of those I have a confidentiality contract. I also work with professional athletes, housewives; professional singers, survivors of rape and different acts of violence. Addicts, Attention Deficit Disorder…the list goes on.

I also work with children, actors, basically anybody who is seeking, searching for the truth. I guide them in finding joy and happiness every moment of every day.

The only reality is perfection… all else is human creation that comes and goes. ONLY God is Perfect, Invincible and Eternal. I choose to create as God in ACTION.

Share your successes with me!!! I have humbly shared my story and gift with you through God's guidance. I would love to hear from you.

Office: (503) 312-0913.
Email: lavoie@masteringyourworld.com

$$[(e^E)\ T]A=O$$
I am the outpicturing of my emotionally driven thoughts and actions

Quotes And Sayings That Inspire

Incurable means curable from within. Disease is the body's way of giving you feedback that you are not loving or grateful.
-Dr. John Demartini

MY NAME IS GOSSIP
(Author Unknown)

I have no respect for justice.
I maim without killing.
I break hearts and ruin lives.

I am cruel and malicious
and gather strength with age

The more I am quoted,
the more I am believed.
I flourish at every level of society.
My victims are helpless.
They cannot protect themselves
against me because
I have no name and no face.

To track me down is impossible.
The harder you try,
the more elusive I become.
I'm nobody's friend.

Once I tarnish a reputation,
it is never the same.
I topple governments
and ruin marriages.
I ruin careers and
cause sleepless nights,

Life ABSOLUTES

Heartache, and indigestion

I spawn suspicion
and generate grief.
I make innocent people
cry in their pillows.
Even my name hisses.

I, AM GOSSIP…Not directed at anyone—just so easy to forget!

Core Values
Acknowledge God as the knower, the doer and the giver at all times
Be God in action…
Know only Love and perfection …Give praise, love and gratitude back to God, my guardian Angel, the Ascended Beings and myself at all times.

"Success lies in the heart, and is activated by the hope that lies in the dream…" -Doug Firebaugh

"When the desire is great enough the solution will appear."
-Karen LaVoie

"Cheerfulness strengthens the heart and makes us persevere in a good life. Therefore the servant of God ought always to be in good spirits." -Saint Philip Neri

Peace Be With YOU!